RISING TO NEW HEIGHTS OF COMMUNICATION AND LEARNING FOR CHILDREN WITH AUTISM

of related interest

Assessing and Developing Communication and Thinking Skills in People with Autism and Communication Difficulties
A Toolkit for Parents and Professionals
Kate Silver
With Autism Initiatives
ISBN 978 1 84310 352 3

Enabling Communication in Children with Autism
Carol Potter and Chris Whittaker
ISBN 978 1 85302 956 1

Communication Issues in Autism and Asperger Syndrome
Do we speak the same language?
Olga Bogdashina
ISBN 978 1 84310 267 0

RISING TO NEW HEIGHTS OF COMMUNICATION AND LEARNING FOR CHILDREN WITH AUTISM

THE DEFINITIVE GUIDE TO USING ALTERNATIVE-AUGMENTATIVE COMMUNICATION, VISUAL STRATEGIES, AND LEARNING SUPPORTS AT HOME AND SCHOOL

CAROL L. SPEARS AND
VICKI L. TURNER

Illustrations by Pete Diaz

Jessica Kingsley Publishers
London and Philadelphia

First published in 2011
by Jessica Kingsley Publishers
116 Pentonville Road
London N1 9JB, UK
and
400 Market Street, Suite 400
Philadelphia, PA 19106, USA

www.jkp.com

Library of Congress Cataloging in Publication Data
A CIP catalog record for this book is available from the Library of Congress

British Library Cataloguing in Publication Data
A CIP catalogue record for this book is available from the British Library

ISBN 978 1 84905 837 7

Printed and bound in United States by
Thomson-Shore, 7300 Joy Road, Dexter, MI 48130

Dedication

It is to the families who have risen above the struggles and challenges of autism, to soar and triumph like the phoenix, that we dedicate this work. It is to educators, therapists, aides, professionals, and other interested parties devoted to improving the lives of children with autism and other developmental disabilities, that we offer this resource guide. All of you have inspired us through your tireless efforts. We hope to facilitate your endeavors.

It is with a promising vision of the future that we dedicate this work to all children diagnosed with autism and other pervasive disabilities. You have touched our souls, and it is in you that we have found our lives' work. It is our intent that this book should be useful to those in your life, making your learning experiences, social situations, and communication efforts more successful.

It is to our husbands, Darren and Hugh, that we dedicate this work. We are truly thankful for the sacrifices you made in order for it to come to fruition. You encouraged, supported, and loved us as you kept the home fires burning to illuminate our journey to completion.

Finally, in all that we do, we acknowledge our Creator who was in the midst of this project from conception to completion. We give all the praise and glory to our Father-Mother-God.

Sincerely,
Carol and Vicki

Contents

List of Figures

List of Boxes

Introduction

Increasing knowledge

A number of words are emotionally laden, but few as much so as the term "autism". Kubler-Ross's (2005) stages of mourning (shock, denial, anger, bargaining, depression, testing, and acceptance) are similarly experienced by families who receive the pronouncement that their children have a pervasive developmental disorder (PDD) of autism or other disability. Hopes, aspirations, goals, and dreams for their children are typically replaced by a grieving process of despair and fear. Fear of the unknown prevails due to a lack of immediately available information, resources, and support. The primary purpose of this introductory chapter is to provide basic information on autism and other PDDs. Second, our aim is to assist families through the final stages of seeking solutions and finding ways to rise above the fear that is often inherent in a diagnosis of developmental disability, communication deficit, or behavior disorders.

If there is any consolation to families, we reveal that some educators, therapists, and other school staff are equally fearful of autism and other pervasive developmental disabilities. The genesis of the emotions may be different, but the underlying cause is the same—fear. We have witnessed many teachers going into shock, not unlike families, when first learning that they are to be assigned a student who has been diagnosed with autism. There is anger and denial that the child has been placed appropriately. This resource guide assists educators, therapists, and other interventionists in rising above the fear of the unknown by providing them with proven effective strategies that facilitate learning, improve behavior, and promote increased communication.

Definitions

The American Psychiatric Association (APA) has designated the category of PDD to indicate children with delay or deviance in their social, language, and/or cognitive development (APA 2000). PDD is not a single disorder, but rather a range of delays of differing magnitude, across different domains. The diagnostic terms that fall within the broad category of PDD include:

- autism spectrum disorder (ASD)
- Asperger syndrome
- Rett's disorder
- childhood disintegrative disorder
- pervasive developmental disorder not otherwise specified (PDD-NOS) (Centers for Disease Control and Prevention 2007; The National Dissemination Center for Children with Disabilities (NICHCY) 2010).

An ASD is a neurological condition affecting a child's ability to comprehend and express language, relate to others, and learn. A diagnosis of PDD-NOS indicates that a child is impaired in the development of reciprocal social interaction or communication, or exhibits stereotyped behavior, but does not meet the criteria for a specific PDD.

According to the APA (2000), the DSM IV-TR diagnostic criteria for an autism disorder are as follows:

A. A total of six (or more) items from (1), (2), and (3), with at least two from (1), and one each from (2) and (3):

    1. Qualitative impairment in social interaction, as manifested by at least two of the following:

        (a) Marked impairment in the use of multiple non-verbal behaviors such as eye-to-eye gaze, facial expression, body postures, and gestures to regulate social interaction.

(b) Failure to develop peer relationships appropriate to developmental level.

(c) A lack of spontaneous seeking to share enjoyment, interests, or achievements with other people (e.g. by a lack of showing, bringing, or pointing out objects of interest).

(d) Lack of social or emotional reciprocity.

2. Qualitative impairments in communication as manifested by at least one of the following:

(a) Delay in, or total lack of, the development of spoken language (not accompanied by an attempt to compensate through alternative modes of communication such as gesture or mime).

(b) In individuals with adequate speech, marked impairment in the ability to initiate or sustain a conversation with others.

(c) Stereotyped and repetitive use of language or idiosyncratic language.

(d) Lack of varied, spontaneous make-believe play or social imitative play appropriate to developmental level.

3. Restricted, repetitive, and stereotyped patterns of behavior, interests, and activities, as manifested by at least one of the following:

(a) Encompassing preoccupation with one or more stereotyped and restricted patterns of interest that is abnormal either in intensity or focus.

(b) Apparently inflexible adherence to specific, nonfunctional routines or rituals.

(c) Stereotyped and repetitive motor manners (e.g. hand or finger flapping or twisting, or complex whole-body movements).

(d) Persistent preoccupation with parts of objects.

B. Delays or abnormal functioning in at least one of the following areas, with onset prior to age three years: (1) social interaction; (2) language as used in social communication; or (3) symbolic or imaginative play.

C. The disturbance is not better accounted for by Rett's disorder or childhood disintegrative disorder.

More simply stated, autism, as defined by the CDC (2007) is one of a group of disorders termed ASDs. ASDs are developmental disabilities that cause significant impairment of social interaction and communication, accompanied by unusual behavior and interests. Although individuals with an ASD may display atypical ways of learning, attending, and reacting to sensory information, their cognitive and learning abilities vary, ranging from gifted to severely challenged. Autism, PDD-NOS and Asperger syndrome, each categorized as an ASD, share some common symptoms but differ in onset, severity, and nature. CDC (2004) define developmental disabilities as a diverse group of severe chronic conditions, resulting in part from mental retardation and/or physical impairments. Individuals affected are challenged by major life activities, such as language, mobility, learning, self-help, and independent living.

Under federal legislation of the Individuals with Disabilities Education Improvement Act (IDEA 2004), infants, toddlers, children, and youth with disabilities receive early intervention, special education, and related services, such as speech-language or occupational therapy. IDEA defines autism as:

> a developmental disability significantly affecting verbal and non-verbal communication and social interaction, generally evident before age three that adversely affects a child's educational performance. Other characteristics often associated with autism are engagement in repetitive activities and stereotyped movements, resistance to environmental change or change in daily routines, and unusual responses to sensory experiences (NICHCY 2010).

What do we currently know?

The questions related to treating autism and other developmental disabilities often appear to outweigh the answers. Research is abundant, yet two primary concerns remain: what causes autism and what is the cure? In *Rising to New Heights*, we do not address either issue. Instead, we respond to the question most frequently asked by families and interventionists: "What do I do for my child or student?" Of the various PDDs, the focus of this text is on autism. The strategies introduced are not applicable solely to autism, however. Families, educators, and interventionists responsible for the care and treatment of children with other developmental disabilities and exceptional needs will also find the information appropriate for home and educational settings. The purpose in writing *Rising to New Heights* was to dispel the fears frequently inherent in a diagnosis of a PDD or other developmental disability. Our approach to accomplishing this complex undertaking was to answer frequently asked questions regarding the influence of autism and other developmental disabilities, communication deficits, and behavior disorders at home and in school.

In Part I, we assist home and school team members in treating a child with a communication disorder due to a PDD, developmental disability, or other condition, to rise to new communicative heights by increasing adults' knowledge of alternative-augmentative communication (AAC). In Part II, we attempt to help teams understand that there is nothing to fear when you use the right supports. The techniques we share involve employing visual strategies to improve communication, behavior, and learning opportunities. Information is provided on using social stories with children with disabilities, and on structuring the environment for their benefit. Finally, in Part III, we further our efforts to help others overcome the fear factor by offering introductory information on various topics including sensory integration, applied behavior analysis (ABA), and routines. We provide additional information on available resources such as national organizations, as well as specific goals and objectives relating to each chapter in this guide.

In Parts I and II, we answer the following questions:

- Who would benefit from a particular intervention or strategy?
- What does the strategy entail?
- Why use the strategy?
- How is the strategy implemented?

- When is the strategy best used (with examples and illustrations)?
- Where does one turn for additional information?

The provision of resources, and goals and objectives, in Part III further supports families and school personnel with information and strategies for overcoming the fear factor. The outcome is success for a child while determining and implementing solutions that work! Improved communication, behavior, and learning come about as the child becomes more easily integrated into home and school activities and functions more effectively.

Expert answers

With increasingly high numbers of children diagnosed daily with a PDD, both private and governmental entities have turned their attention to learning more regarding the disorders. The CDC responds to questions about who is affected by ASDs by reporting that the condition occurs in all racial, ethnic, and socio-economic groups (CDC 2009). ASDs occur four times more often in boys than girls. The CDC's recent studies indicate that in 2009 approximately 1 in 110 eight year old children in several regions of the United States had an ASD (CDC 2009). According to the CDC, autism can be detected in children as young as 18 months of age. Children in high-risk groups, such as siblings of those previously diagnosed, or children of parents with autism, should be monitored closely for acquisition of developmental milestones or warning signs of an ASD or other developmental disabilities. The CDC lists specific behaviors as "possible red flags" for an ASD. These are when children:

- do not play "pretend" games (e.g. pretend to "feed" a doll)
- do not point at objects to show interest (e.g. point at an airplane flying over)
- do not look at objects when another person points at them
- have trouble relating to others, or not have an interest in other people at all
- avoid eye contact and want to be alone

- have trouble understanding other people's feelings or talking about their own feelings

- prefer not to be held or cuddled, or might cuddle only when they want to

- appear to be unaware when other people talk to them, but respond to other sounds

- appear to be very interested in people, but not know how to talk to, play with, or relate to them

- repeat or echo words or phrases said to them, or repeat words or phrases in place of normal language (echolalia)

- have trouble expressing their needs using typical words or motions

- repeat actions over and over again

- have trouble adapting to changes in routine

- have unusual reactions to the way things smell, taste, look, feel, or sound

- lose skills once displayed (e.g. stop saying words they were once using) (CDC 2007).

Although information exists on the prevalence and symptoms of autism, research on causes is not as specific. According to the CDC, scientists believe that both genetics and the environment have an influence on ASDs. There are probably many factors that can lead to autism. There is speculation that a child's diet, inoculations, or mercury may be responsible. As stated previously, our emphasis is not on the *why* of developmental disabilities, but rather on *what to do*, particularly in order to remove the factor of fear from the equation.

Especially for parents

As we formulated ideas for this definitive guide, our imaging of a hot air balloon typified numerous situations that we encountered during our decades of providing services to children with disabilities and their home and school teams. On the one hand, the balloon represents escalating emotions, when filled with the hot air of fear, anxiety, and dread that often emerge when parents are given a diagnosis of autism or other disability. The balloon rises at the onset of mourning and extinguishes hopes and dreams for their children. Shock, denial, anger, bargaining, and depression keep the emotional balloon afloat. But we strive to rescue such wayward balloons, not by deflating them but rather by putting families and school members in control. With appropriate information, teams learn to release the emotional hot air and replace it instead with new knowledge and strategies we know work. This alternate view of the hot air balloon depicts families and educational teams at the helm, with information, effective methods, and resources fueling the apparatus to rise above fear. Families, in particular, need to know they are not on a solitary flight. They are embarking on a journey replete, certainly, with challenges; but most significantly, with this text as a guide, they are also choosing a path of success for their children.

Readers are encouraged to move beyond the initial mourning stages to those of testing new solutions, and accepting and implementing what works best for their children or students. Be mindful that all individuals are different, with unique interests, skills, and talents. The core strategies presented in this book, nonetheless, are intended to guide intervention approaches at home and school. We intend that *Rising to New Heights* should make the trip smoother, and that the destination should be one of enhanced communication, learning, behavior, and functioning for children living with developmental and other disabilities

Further reading

American Psychiatric Association (APA) (2000) *Diagnostic Criteria for 229.00 Autistic Disorder (DSM-IV-TR)*. Arlington, VA: APA.

Center for Disease Control and Prevention (CDC) (2004) *What Are Developmental Disabilities?* Available at www.cdc.gov/ncbddd/dd/default.htm. Accessed August 2010.

Center for Disease Control and Prevention (CDC) (2007). www.cdc.gov/ncbdd/autism/signs.html. Accessed 12 January 2009.

Center for Disease Control and Prevention (CDC) (2009) CDC Press Briefing on Autism Surveillance Summary. Available at www.cdc.gov/media/transcripts/2009/t091218.htm. Accessed 2 July 2010.

Kubler-Ross, E. and Kessler, D. (2005) *On Grief and Grieving*. Sribner, NY: NY.

National Dissemination Center for Children with Disablilities (NICHCY) (2010). www.nichcy.org

PART I

Alternative-Augmentative Communication Methods

Imagine initiating an exchange with another individual, only to discover yourself suddenly silent...wordless...voiceless. A myriad of ideas swirl in your head. You might even hear them loud and clear; yet, the person with whom you seek to interact has no awareness of your meaning or your intent. In effect, you have experienced a communication breakdown, a commonplace occurrence for a child on the autism spectrum or with a pervasive developmental disability. We wrote Part I of *Rising to New Heights* because we recognized the frustration of children with disabilities who lack sufficient means to communicate effectively. Also, in Part I, we offer support to adults who deal with their own fears regarding how children with severe disorders communicate.

Communication is the ability to relay information and thoughts using a reliable method of expression that produces a mutually understood message intentionally exchanged between two or more people. Challenges arise when an educator or parent attempts to communicate with a child who has significant limitations in expressive communication abilities, resulting in inconsistencies in message production and poor intelligibility. Typically, verbalizations are not the only method of expression: gestures, intonation patterns, facial expressions, and posturing may also relay meaning to the listener. In Part I of *Rising*, we answer Who, What, Why, How, Where, and When questions about utilizing and expanding an individual's methods of expression and application of alternative methods of communication to relay mutually understood messages. Instruction on Alternative Augmentative Communication (AAC) techniques to compensate for the limitations in message generation, and to provide individualized methods that allow a child's ability to engage and be successful in the communication process, is discussed.

Communication is a necessity when individuals attempt to transfer information, have wants and needs met, create social bonds, understand the environment, control their circumstances, and realize their self-worth. AAC strategies are implemented to assist in bridging the gap in social, educational, interpersonal, and professional settings for individuals with expressive communication limitations. When one takes on the task of working with individuals who must compensate for limited expressive abilities, there are many variables to consider, such as cognitive levels, physical abilities, typical communicative partners, and communicative needs. As detailed in Part I, these variables dictate the specific AAC strategies and communicative supports required to address the specific communicative needs of the students.

The chapters in Part I of *Rising* address topics of AAC highlighting our knowledge and experiences in effective, functional use of AAC. As authors, our goal for all readers of these chapters is to be able to:

- utilize alternative assessment procedures to identify the specific communicative needs of the student

- become familiar with various AAC options that compensate for significant expressive communication delays

- tailor AAC goals, strategies, materials, and equipment for each student addressed.

1 | SPEECH GENERATING DEVICES

Who would benefit from the use of speech generating devices (SGDs)?

Individuals with severe expressive communication disorders benefit most from the use of SGDs. Included among these individuals are those who utilize gesture, speech and/or written communication methods that do not adequately address their expressive communication attempts or needs. In all these individuals, the primary cause for the limitations in expressive communication should not be due to hearing impairment. Many individuals are capable of some verbal output; however, their utterances are limited and inadequate to meet their varied communication needs (START 1996). Candidates for AAC vary in disabilities and may include individuals with autism, cognitive or developmental delay, traumatic brain injury, cerebral palsy, specific language disabilities, developmental apraxia, muscular dystrophy, and sensory impairments.

What are SGDs?

SGDs are communication devices that offer speech output, have programming capabilities, and can provide the individual with a broader range of communication possibilities (although this is not necessarily the case) (START 1996).

There are two types of SGDs. Systems designed for the single use of speech output are called dedicated systems. An example of a dedicated system is the Vantage Lite (manufactured by Prentke Romich Company). The second type of SGD is a computer system that is used for a variety of functions including that of generating speech. Examples of this type of SGD system is the Mercury (manufactured by Assistive Technology Inc.) and a computer with Speaking Dynamically software installed (START 1996).

The dedicated systems range from the one message voice output device, such as the Big Mack (manufactured by Ablenet Inc.), to the mid-range devices, such as the Go Talk, Communication Builder, and Tech Talk, to the high-tech devices, such as the ECO-2 (manufactured by Prentke Romich Company), the V (manufactured by DynaVox Electronics Inc.), and ComLink (manufactured by Forbes Rehab Services Inc.).

Why are SGDs used in the classroom setting?

Over the years, new legislation addressing issues relating to special needs students has prompted change in the educational opportunities for such students. According to Hartsell and McIntosh (2005), federal and state mandates dictate that students with cognitive or developmental delay, cerebral palsy, autism, specific language disabilities, multiple disabilities, sensory impairments, developmental apraxia, muscular dystrophy, and traumatic brain injury, receive free and appropriate education in the least restricted environment. Included in the mandates is the necessity for public school systems to provide each student with the specific materials or equipment needed for them to successfully access the curriculum. Students with significant communication difficulties are faced with the daily challenge of functioning effectively in the educational environment with the inability to relay even the simplest of messages. SGDs are therefore used to bridge the gap that poor expressive communication abilities create in the academic setting. When SGDs are effectively integrated into the classroom curriculum, students have the tools that they need to be productive, independent, and successful learners. Technology provides the students with the tools that they need to participate and achieve within these educational activities.

How should SGDs be integrated in the classroom?

No SGD is a "cure" for an ineffective or inadequate expressive communication system. Rather, an SGD should be considered one component of a communication system that allows a student to effectively relay messages. There will certainly be occasions when the use of just one SGD will not be appropriate in a communication setting. It is therefore incumbent upon the educators to develop and teach the student an arsenal of communication strategies. Once equipped with multiple options for expressive communication, the student can in turn pair the most effective and efficient method with the communication situation at home and school. This allows for faster and easier communication exchanges, more communication opportunities, and more learning. (Downey *et al.* 2004).

Important factors to consider when using SGDs

Irrespective of the SGD considered for a student, it is important to remember some basic premises (START 1996):

- SGDs enhance speech and language development.

- Communication efforts are more effective when additional materials and techniques are used in conjunction with an SGD.

- Formal training and support in device use fosters more accurate use of the SGD in all communicative settings.

- Educators maintain verbal modeling when communicating with a student using an SGD.

- Ideally, the educational team participating in the evaluation and selection process should consist of any combination of the following members:
  - speech-language pathologist
  - occupational therapist
  - physical therapist
  - itinerant teacher for visually impaired
  - special education teacher

23

- o classroom or subject teacher
- o computer or augmentative communication specialist
- o parent
- o student

- Some students use negative behaviors as a form of communication. When addressing the behaviors, it is important that they are not immediately dismissed but are analyzed to determine if the displayed behavior is an inappropriate yet purposeful communication attempt.

- The SGD system should be a functional one. The content of the system should reflect the child's cognitive level, physical abilities, interests, and communication needs.

- When changes and additions are needed to supplement the child's language needs, re-programming the SGD should be easy.

- A viable successful communication method should not be replaced with a more abstract time-consuming SGD. That is, the students who are able to nod and shake their head for yes and no should not be directed to use a device for yes and no.

- Students need frequent opportunities to use their SGD, particularly during the early stages of learning.

- More success in learning is often achieved when a student realizes that the SGD offers pleasurable outcomes such as control, having desired needs met, social interaction, and fun.

- Teaching the use of a SGD should be done in interesting, naturalistic settings rather than through memorization and drill.

- Use of the SGD should be incorporated throughout all communicative settings (i.e., home, school, work).

- The educational team needs to be prepared to commit the time and energy needed for successful teaching of the use of the SGD.

When should SGDs be used?

An SGD may be used when:

- there is a communicative situation and the desire to communicate

- the potential user has the ability to formulate a message cognitively and to understand and use a device

- an SGD has been determined a viable alternative means of communication by a speech-language pathologist following an AAC evaluation

- there is a need to relay messages during academic lessons, provide information and questions about vocational responsibilities during social exchanges, and to relay wants and needs when needed.

It is paramount, however, that SGDs are used following specific training on their purpose, function, and operation. Teaching the use of SGDs for communication takes lots of time and patience by the user, family, teacher, and other students. When teaching the SGD, there are multiple methods that may be used and important factors that should be considered. (CeDIR 2003).

The educational team at the school develops a plan on when the students are to use their communication method. Within this plan, the team determines when and how often the communication tool is to be used, what vocabulary is needed, who will program or fabricate whatever is required and what the expectations of the students are. There follows examples of how an SGD can be incorporated during different times of the day. Keep in mind that the expectations for expressive output are first and foremost dependent on the vocabulary constraints of the device. After that, familiarity with the device and cognitive level also contribute in determining the level of expectation. Consequently, the following activities may vary depending on the device used. For example, some students may use their SGD to label the food items they want at mealtime, while others will use yes or no in response to food items already labeled, in order to indicate what they want. In both cases, however, the student is requesting food items.

Burns (2005) identified classroom settings as priceless opportunities or costly obstacles to building proficient use of SGDs, citing student, teacher, and peer participation as pivotal factors in helping promote the use of devices. Below, he identifies the three levels of participation required to encourage AAC users to seek the many opportunities for activities to develop communication skills.

When student participation is a factor

This level of participation recognizes the student as the focal point. There are four primary areas for student participation:

- social interaction
- curricular interaction
- communication personality
- communication technique.

These four areas of participation will certainly have an impact on the individual user's desire and need to use a device.

Social interaction

According to Burns (2005), opportunities for social interaction exist in infinite quantities for verbal children at school and at home. These interactions are generally short in duration and they are often not school-related even though they occur in school. Social interactions occur before, after, and during structured school, home, and community activities. It is therefore recommended to include some social vocabulary on an SGD unless it is not a high priority either because of limits on the amount of vocabulary that can be included on the SGD, or because it is not deemed important by the SGD user.

Figures 1.1–1.6 are examples of different SGDs that are programmed with vocabulary for communication during social situations. For example, Figures 1.1 and 1.2 show SGDs with greetings to staff and peers on arrival at school, and Figures 1.3 and 1.4 show SGDs with messages to allow for communication regarding arrival topics. Figures 1.5 and 1.6 demonstrate how students can be helped to respond to possible questions on arrival such as:

Figure 1.1 Greeting on arrival at school (a)

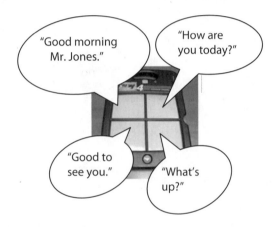

Figure 1.2 Greeting on arrival at school (b)

Figure 1.3 Communicating on arrival (a)

Figure 1.4 Communicating on arrival (b)

Figure 1.5 Answering questions on arrival (a)

Figure 1.6 Answering questions on arrival (b)

Do you want breakfast?

Are you hot?

What would you like for breakfast?

When including vocabulary for social situations, it is important to keep in mind that reasonable speed for message generation is critical. Message generation that is so slow that it creates non-functional communication by impeding or stopping the flow of communication should be addressed by creating easier access. Efficiency of access to vocabulary is critical and may require using one word, a short phrase or, at the most, very concise sentences when communicating during social settings.

Curricular interaction

Communication opportunities exist during structured class activities embedded in the school day. Typical school activities such as reading groups, circle time, show and tell, and oral reports provide opportunities for expressive language. The level and type of expressive opportunities are dependent upon the type of classes in which the student is enrolled, the make-up of the classroom, and the developmental level of the student. It is therefore important to recognize the communication opportunities and teach the student to use the SGD to communicate successfully in the school environment (Burns 2005).

Figures 1.7–1.9 are examples of devices with programmed messages that can be used during structured activities at home or at school. The student with an SGD that provides these types of messages, and who has been trained on the use of the SGD, now has the potential to independently respond, interact, and successfully access the curriculum in the least restrictive environment.

For example, Figure 1.7 shows how students can participate in typical group weather activities. Figure 1.8 shows how students may respond to structured group questions such as:

- How old are you?
- Who do you want to be your helper?
- Whose turn is it?

- How many girls are here today?
- How old are you?
- What color is my shirt?

Figure 1.9 shows how SGDs can enable a student to:

- request basic wants and needs in the classroom
- ask questions to request help
- request additional materials
- make comments.

SGDs can also help students to participate in home activities by making choices, giving structured responses, naming vocabulary items, and expressing vocabulary during repetitive books.

Communication personality

Communication personality considers the specific attributes of a student's personality when determining use of an SGD. As with verbal students, there are extroverted and introverted AAC users. Students exhibit varied levels of desire to speak in a classroom environment irrespective of their ability to generate messages on their device. Some students seek the center of attention and will communicate freely in the classroom setting while others prefer not to interact. These same

Figure 1.7 Weather

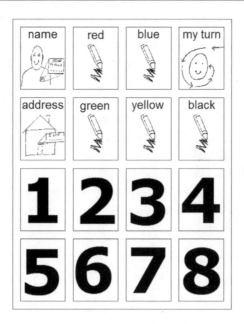

Figure 1.8 Circle or group time

Figure 1.9 Interaction in the classroom

attributes should be considered when using a device. The need and desire to communicate, and in what settings, are variables to consider when determining appropriate device use and vocabulary.

It is also important to remember to use content vocabulary as well as comment vocabulary. Most speakers interject related comments when communicating for various purposes. Neglecting to include these comments often strips individuals of personality when speaking. Comments about how they feel add motivation, interest, and personality to the device users' communication (Burns 2005).

Figures 1.10–1.12 offer overlays that may be used in SGDs that include appropriate comments for the topics. For example, at meal or snack time, students can:

- request food items
- ask for help
- indicate when more is desired
- indicate when finished
- make general comment about food items.

In free time students can:

- make choice of desired activity
- make comments or requests about activity. For example, during a bubble-blowing activity, the student can make comments such as "pop it", or "big bubble"
- Integrate self into activity by using messages such as "my turn", he's cheating", and "I'm next".

Communication technique

Communication technique involves how the SGD is used and affects the speed of communication. SGD users who know how to access vocabulary are more adept in their communication. Those who are not familiar with their device may have a difficult time generating desired messages within a reasonable time. They may become discouraged when impatient communication partners interrupt or respond prior to message completion. It is therefore essential to teach the use, purpose, function, and operation of the device to ensure maximum communicative success (Burns 2005).

Figure 1.10 Meal or snack time

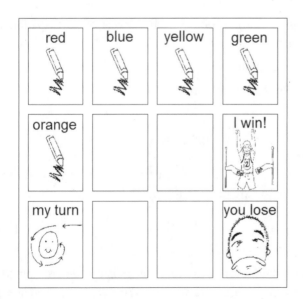

Figure 1.11 Free time (a)

Figure 1.12 Free time (b)

When teacher participation is a factor

According to Burns (2005), teacher levels of participation involve three primary areas:

- Teaching activity.
- Communication activity.
- Peer activity.

These individual levels focus on teaching language skills, creating opportunities for communication in a natural environment, and allowing activities with peers to promote familiarity with the device and make it an extension of the user's personality rather than a toy or high-tech gadget.

Teaching activity

Teaching activities for device users include, but are not limited to, the classroom assignments presented to all the students in a class. All too often, SGD users are handed a device and expected to communicate. This is done when many non-verbal students have deficits in language abilities as well as limited knowledge on where and how to find words on the device. Devices can be set up, if properly planned, to incorporate lesson-plan material for student participation in the classroom while they are learning to use the device more effectively (Burns 2005).

Communication activity

Communication activities may include show and tell, oral book reports, games, and story telling. These kinds of activities provide opportunities for long varied language utterances that can be pre-planned and rehearsed. Additionally, students are provided with the opportunity for inclusion in talk time activities along with classmates providing practice with SGDs. Being the caller in a Bingo game or playing a game of Uno can offer varied, yet predictable, opportunities for expression.

Figure 1.13 is an example of a Bingo overlay that may be used in an SGD. Figure 1.14 is an overlay that offers vocabulary for communicating information between school and home.

The messages can be elaborate, describing activities or events that occurred at school. They can also be as simple as using the SGD to let parents know to look in the book bag for a note from the teacher. Students can also use the device to:

- request desired food items
- indicate when they are hungry
- express when more is desired
- choose a TV program to watch
- express feelings
- express need for help.

Peer activity

Peer activities utilize other students as communicative partners. Including the students' friends as in expressive language activities offers a less threatening, more fun opportunity to use SGDs. The student is in a more casual and comfortable situation, removed from the sense of being tested and timed, and released from the fear of

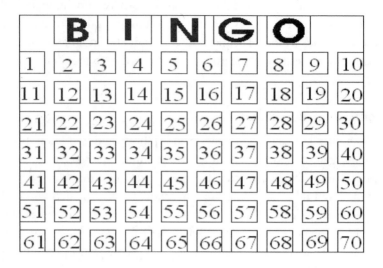

Figure 1.13 Bingo

Figure 1.14 Messages from school to home

providing a wrong answer. Group and playtime activities offer many opportunities for communication and fun. SGDs should include commands and fun statements based on the activity.

When peer participation is a factor

Peers throughout the school, at home, or in the community may be used for dual purposes. Peer activity and classroom involvement are affected at this participation level. Peers may include classmates as well as same-aged peers throughout the school and community. Verbal students from clubs or extracurricular groups may engage in activities with the SGD user. AAC users may find they can be more involved in student activities with help from verbal peers.

Where can you get help?

Burns, C. (2005) *Classroom AAC: Communication through Participation.* Contact author at craig@a2csolutionsgroup.com to request this publication.

CeDIR (Center for Disability Information and Referral) (2003) *Augmentative and Alternative Communication Introduction.* Available at www.rehabtool.com/forum/discussions/98.html, accessed on 15 June 2009.

Downey, D., Daugherty, P., Helt, S. and Daugherty, D. (2004) "Integrating AAC into the classroom: low-tech strategies." *Asha Leader,* 21 September, pp.6–7, 36.

Hartsell, K. and McIntosh, K. (2005) "Integrating assistive technology into the general education curriculum for students with high incidence disabilities." *Closing the Gap 24,* 3, 4–6, 36.

START (Special Needs Technology Assessment Resource Support Team) (1996) *Meeting the Needs of Students with Communication Difficulties.* Berwick, NS: Annapolis Valley Regional School Board. Available at www.nsnet.org/start/communication.pdf, accessed on 15 June 2009.

2 | PICTURE EXCHANGE COMMUNICATION SYSTEM (PECS)

Who uses the Picture Exchange Communication System (PECS)?

The Picture Exchange Communication System (PECS) was originally developed at the Delaware Autistic Program for children with autism. When it was originated, its primary purpose was to teach children with autism to initiate communication. Subsequently, it has been found that PECS is appropriate for individuals who are non-verbal as well as those with limited expressive language. This group includes those with phonetic problems, apraxia, few communicative partners, or no initiation (Wallin 2004). The system can be implemented successfully with children as young as two years of age.

What is PECS?

PECS is an augmentative communication system designed to facilitate quick, effective, functional communication. Vicker (2002) describes it as a modified applied behavior analysis program established to teach non-verbal symbolic communication. It is a concrete visual-based program that does not require the more difficult motor planning that many signs in sign language require. Although speech emerges with some individuals and verbal speech is indirectly encouraged, PECS is not specifically designed to teach speech. Its primary objective is to establish an understanding about the purpose and method of communication exchanges, and to facilitate communication by providing the opportunity to relay messages through pictures.

Why use PECS?

The initial suggestion to parents to use PECS with their child often evokes hesitancy, disappointment, and disagreement stemming from their conception that the use of this communication system means their child will never talk, or that speech will no longer be addressed. This is discouraging for parents because the hope that their child will someday talk is immediately destroyed, and the fear that their child will never talk is affirmed. Research demonstrates the opposite is true. The implementation of PECS can enhance a student's language development (Frost and Bondy 2002). PECS has many advantages including the following:

- Communication exchanges are clearly intentional and readily understood.

- Interactions are initiated by the student, thereby eliminating prompt dependency.

- Exchanges are meaningful and motivating.

- Materials are inexpensive, simple to fabricate, and portable.

- A communicative partner does not need specific training to understand a message. Anyone willing to participate in an exchange is a potential communicative partner. The student therefore has few limits in communicative opportunities (Wallin 2004).

How does PECS work?

During implementation of each of the six phases in PECS, an individual chooses a picture from a variety available, then gives the picture to a communication partner. Knowing the individual's request, the partner can then provide the requested item or fulfill a desired need.

According to Frost and Bondy (2002), the six phases of PECS are:

Phase I. Purpose: To initiate communication

During the first phase, a facilitator and message receiver is needed to work with the child. The child is presented with a previously determined desired item. When the desired item is presented and the child reaches for it, the facilitator physically redirects the child's reach to the picture of the item and assists them in picking up the picture and giving it to the message receiver in exchange for the item. Physical guidance by the facilitator is gradually faded. The goal of the PECS is to teach spontaneous initiation of communication and not to prompt responses to our requests. It is therefore important to resist talking too much. Phrases with, "give me" should never be used for they teach one step directions rather than spontaneous initiation of a response. The desired item is to motivate the picture exchange. The facilitator physically demonstrates the process and very little language is needed. Figure 2.1 on p.42 depicts the picture exchange process implemented with the student and two helpers.

Phase II. Purpose: To teach distance and persistence

A PECS book or board is provided with one picture presented at a time. During this phase, PECS users are taught to move longer distances to complete exchanges for a desired item. They are taught to locate their book or board and move longer distances to communication partners for the exchange. Figure 2.2 on p.43 depicts the use of one picture in the beginning stages of picture exchange.

Phase III. Purpose: To discriminate between pictures or symbols

A desirable is paired with a non-desirable on communication book. The child exchanges using one of the pictures and receives the requested item. When the desired item is exchanged, the child receives the item and social reinforcement from the message receiver. When the non-desired item is exchanged, they receive that item and error correction steps are taken. The message receiver may ask, "What do you want?" or the facilitator may physically prompt the child to the desired picture. Once the child increases accuracy in discriminating between two items, additional items are gradually added. Figure 2.3 on p.44 depicts multiple PECS pictures set up with an item that is desirable for the user along with a non-desirable or neutral item to facilitate discrimination.

Phase IV. Purpose: To begin using sentence structure

Icons for carrier phrase, "I want" are provided as sentence starters to be combined with a picture request. A sentence strip is with the sentence starter added to the front of the PECS book and the child learns to build a sentence by adding the desired picture to the strip and exchanging the entire strip. The message receiver then turns the strip toward the student and reads the phrase and provides the child with the desired item. Figure 2.4 on p.45 depicts the use of a sentence structure format with the pictures.

Phase V. Purpose: To answer a direct question

The student is taught to answer the question, "What do you want?". The use of additional words may be taught during this phrase to refine message meaning. For example, the child may replace "I want lego", with "I want red lego".

Phase VI. Purpose: To begin to develop commenting

The child learns to communicate more than just their wants and needs. During this phase, the purpose for exchanges no longer is only for requesting. Exchanges for the purposes of commenting and providing information are now taught by using the carrier phrases, "I see" and "I have". Icons for "I see" and "I hear" are introduced one at a time on the communication board in a systematic fashion.

(Frost and Bondy 2002)

When do you implement PECS?

It is appropriate to use PECS when addressing the expressive communicative needs of individuals who are non-verbal, primarily echolalic, or have unintelligible speech, and those who have only a small set of meaningful words or signs in their repertoire. PECS is used when addressing many communicative needs and when working with various populations. The training is not limited by age and can be offered to an adult with a cognitive impairment as well as to a young child with no cognitive impairments (Vicker 2002).

PECS is often introduced to students with autism; however, it is not limited to this population. Careful consideration of the program and its strengths and weaknesses should play an important role in program selection for each prospective communication learner.

There is a small set of criteria that helps determine when PECS may be used (Vicker 2002).

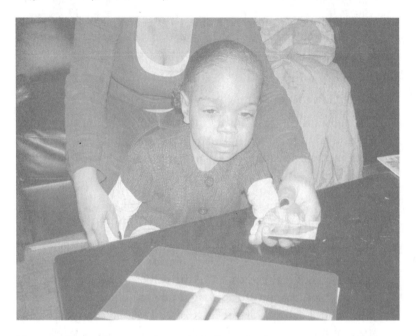

Figure 2.1 Phase 1 Picture exchange (a) In Figure 2.1 the communicator (child) is being physically prompted by the facilitator to exchange a picture with the message receiver. The physical prompts are faded as soon as possible.

Intention to communicate

The candidate for PECS training should demonstrate at least some instances of intention to communicate by trying to gain attention in conjunction with a purposeful communicative attempt. The child who pulls another person to a desired object has at least some understanding of intentionality. Those who make attempts and

Figure 2.2 Phase 2 Picture exchange (b) Figure 2.2 shows training in the exchange of pictures when a desired item is placed on top of the communication binder while opportunities are created to encourage multiple trials for the communicator to exchange the picture. The communicator is then taught to locate the binder and travel to the message receiver.

gestures to acquire a desire or need without purposefully gaining, or checking to see if they have, the attention of another, may not be intentional and may need a different approach before PECS training.

Interests and preferences

It is important that the child demonstrates interests and preferences, along with having intentionality. PECS helps to teach the concept of the purpose and power of alternative communication.

If the individual displays few or no interests that will facilitate a desire to communicate, it may be more difficult to understand and learn the purpose and power of effective alternative communication while using PECS. Identifying preferences is a first step before beginning PECS training. It is beneficial to list interests and dislikes of various types of foods, activities, or items through informal assessments prior to initiating PECS.

43

Picture discrimination ability

In Figure 2.3 a desired item is placed on the top of the binder with a non-desired item to facilitate discrimination between pictures. Additional pictures are introduced as discrimination abilities improve.

Picture discrimination ability is not required for accurate use of PECS although individuals with good discrimination skills may progress faster initially. There are other individuals who have spontaneously demonstrated that they can already discriminate pictured material and already know how to use pictures to communicate. These are individuals who are indicating their desires by finding pictures within their environment and taking them to a message receiver independently. Those observed doing this may benefit from different AAC programs that would allow for the generation of an increased number of new and more complex messages. (Vicker 2002).

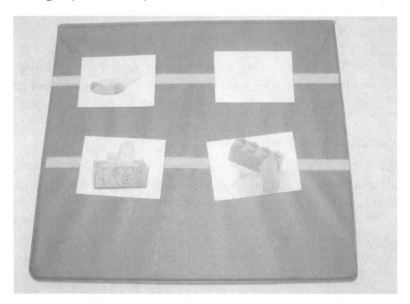

Figure 2.3 Phase 3 Picture discrimination

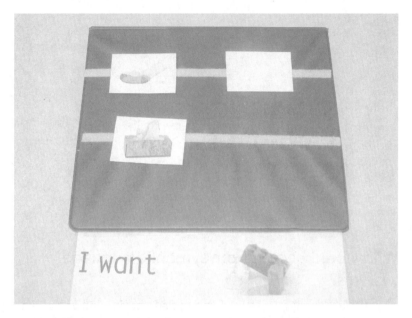

Figure 2.4 Phase 4 "I want" The phrase "I want" is used as a sentence starter to introduce sentence structure. The communicator completes the phrase with the desired item and exchanges the complete phrase.

Where can you get help?

Frost, L.A. and Bondy, A. (2002) *The Picture Exchange Communication System Training Manual.* Newark, DE: Pyramid Educational Products Inc.

Vicker, B. (2002) *What is the Picture Exchange Communication System or PECS?* Available at www.isdd.indiana.edu/irca/communication/whatisthepec.html, accessed on 26 June 2009.

Wallin, J. (2004) *Visual Supports: PECS.* Available at www.polyxo.com/visualsupport/pecs.html, accessed on 26 June 2009.

W
H
E
R
E

3 | SYMBOLIC LANGUAGE SYSTEMS

WHO

Who would benefit from symbolic language systems?

A symbolic language system is appropriate for any individual who exhibits limited expressive and receptive communication abilities. Anyone who cannot relay messages with enough intelligibility for the listener to understand would benefit from the use of symbolic language systems. This type of communication method is appropriate to augment or replace the expressive and receptive communication for a wide range of individuals with minimum to complex communication needs. Symbolic language systems vary in complexity, use, and structure and are individualized to meet the cognitive, physical, communicative and social needs of the user. It is therefore not limited to a particular population offering benefits to many. Anyone who possesses the ability to discriminate and interpret visual representations may use a type of symbolic language system. It is also important to note that individuals who use another communication system as their primary expressive method may also benefit from a symbolic language system to supplement their communication.

WHAT

What is a symbolic language system?

We define symbolic language systems as any method of communication that utilizes an action or material, assigns specific messages to it, and uses it consistently to relay meaning to the listener. A symbolic language system, a type of AAC, provides a consistent and easy-to-interpret method of relaying messages when a verbal message cannot be presented intelligibly. Pictures of items or places, labels of products, objects, gestures, and vocalizations are most commonly used to depict representations of desired messages. The type of symbol used is dependent upon the skills, abilities, and preferences of the individual. Objects provide a more concrete representation of the desired message that is often easier for the communicator to understand, but less concrete, more abstract materials, such as photographs, line drawings, symbols, and printed words, may also be used to represent the desired message.

Symbolic language systems offer the individual with limited communication skills an organized, simplistic, readily available way to relay functional and desired messages. There are many types of symbolic language systems. Each system is customized to the specific, cognitive, communication, social, and physical needs of the user. One way of rising above the fear factor associated with communicating with a child who has limited expressive abilities is to equip the child with a symbolic language system. The following are descriptions of some of the most commonly used symbolic language systems.

Communication page

The communication page is a topic-specific page of symbols to relay messages with a variety of partners in different environments. Vocabulary necessary for the topic of the page is combined on one sheet. Sample topics might include a restaurant order page, circle time vocabulary page, TV channel or program choice page, or student personal information page.

Figure 3.1, on p.56 is an example of a communication page. These pages are used to communicate rapid, simple, predictable vocabulary during appropriate communicative settings.

Communication board

The communication board is a single-layer type of symbolic language system that offers varied vocabulary within boundaries. It differs from a communication page in that the vocabulary is not topic-specific and vocabulary options are limited to the space available on the board.

The board contains grids where pictures are inserted to represent messages. The vocabulary is typically separated by parts of speech to provide an easier method of vocabulary identification and message generation. The communication board user points to pictures to relay messages. Figure 3.4 on p.60 is an example of a communication board. An advantage of the communication board is that all of the vocabulary options are available in this one location and page turning or other physical manipulation is not needed to access vocabulary. This is significant for the individual who exhibits limitations in gross and fine motor abilities. A disadvantage to using communication boards is that the messages the user can generate is limited by the size of the board and the number of pictures that can be displayed.

Communication binder

The communication binder is often a three-ring notebook that contains sheets to which communication symbols may be attached. The sheets are typically a collection of communication pages in that each sheet within the binder is a topic-specific page of symbols to communicate messages for a communicative situation. The pages being organized by topic or category assist the user in the ease of locating desired symbols. The binder may be created to have as many or as few pages as the individual can physically and cognitively handle. The vocabulary is dependent on the communicative desires and needs of the individual. Figure 3.5 has examples of vocabulary separated by category on communication pages that may be included in a communication binder.

Communication wallet

The communication wallet is similar to the communication binder but smaller. The wallet provides categorized pages of vocabulary in a smaller wallet size so it can be transported more readily.

Symbolic communication methods are not limited to picture-based materials. Other representations are classified under the umbrella of symbolic language systems. Any method that gives a specific communicative meaning to a previously general or generic item or action is a type of symbolic language system.

Objects

Using objects to represent a message is one of the most concrete symbolic language systems. They are easier for some individuals to interpret and understand. Generally, an object commonly used or associated with the desired message is presented as a symbol for the message. For example, a spoon is used to represent "eat" and a CD is used to represent "listen to music". Objects are sometimes bulky, making it more difficult, cumbersome, or unrealistic to always have them readily available. A portion or piece of an object may be used when actual items are too large to use as an expressive representation for a message. A few pieces of a chain link may be used to represent "I want to go on the swing" and a swatch of a towel to represent "I want to take a bath". A shortcoming with objects is that it is difficult to represent some abstract messages with an object. A common desire for many individuals is to express "leave me alone". Finding an object to adequately represent this message is challenging.

Sign language

Sign language is a system that employs gestures made with the hands and other cues, including facial expressions and postures of the body. The use of this structured language system provides a comprehensive, rapid method of communication. A disadvantage of sign language is that it is complex, requiring learned knowledge in order to interpret it. Any communication partner unfamiliar with sign language will not comprehend the message.

Gestures

The use of gestures is a crude method of communication that is used to relay messages learned between the communicator and the partner. Any movement that is consistently used for specific desired messages and is learned by the communication partner can be considered a type of gestural symbolic language system. The inability of unfamiliar partners to interpret some gestures, and the limitation of the number of gestures that can be consistently used, are a couple of the shortcomings of this method.

Vocal approximations

Often individuals with speech impairments do not have the ability to execute the intricate fine motor movements of the articulators and coordinate them with respiration in order to render intelligible speech. These same individuals, however, often do possess the ability to produce distinct variations in their vocalizations. Varied vocalizations may be used consistently for specific messages. Just as in gestures, any vocalization that is consistently used for specific desired messages and is learned by the communication partner can be considered a symbolic language system. The disadvantages of vocal approximations mirror those of gestures in that unfamiliar listeners who have not learned the patterns of the approximations cannot interpret them. Individuals who rely on this method of communication are also limited in the number of vocal approximations that can be included in their communicative repertoire.

Why use a symbolic language system?

The ability to use symbols for expressive and receptive communication is a valuable skill for individuals with severe cognitive and speech disabilities (Stephenson and Linfoot 1996). Symbolic language systems are used to develop and facilitate communication during structured and unstructured settings. There are multiple reasons to use symbolic language systems. Three of the most common reasons are as follows.

Easy to access materials

A perfectly effective and efficient symbolic language system may be created using as little as paper, glue, common objects, and pictures from magazines or product containers. We worked with preschool teachers who saved the paper lids from different cereal bowl containers. These paper lids were presented to enable the students to choose the cereal they desired. A message page may also be produced using magazine pictures or actual objects that represent a message (e.g. spoon for "eat," ball for "play," small pillow for "go to bed"). Computer software that allows for rapid and specific generation of pictures to be used in symbolic language systems are also available. Some of the more popular software titles include "Boardmaker" and "Picture This". The internet is also a convenient source of free representations. The images section of the Google website (www.google.com) contains photographs, line drawings and other illustrations that may be used when fabricating symbolic language systems. Photographs of real objects with which a child is familiar may also be used to communicate messages in symbolic language systems.

Minimum cost to produce

Not only are the materials used in symbolic language systems easy to access, they are usually cost effective too. The cost to generate materials can be minimal, as with the cereal bowl lids that teachers and families might collect, or the development of digital photos that represent desired messages. Symbolic representations may be drawn, common objects that are already owned may be collected, or images may be downloaded free from the internet. These free and low-cost options for symbol generation provide the materials needed to create an effective and efficient communication system.

Useful as secondary communication system

At times, symbolic communication systems are easier to access and have the capacity to generate messages faster than other AAC options. A child who uses a speech generating device (SGD) has the advantage of being able to produce more complex novel messages compared to a symbolic language system. However, the SGD generally needs additional time to set up and complete the multiple activations required to generate one message. Symbolic communication systems can relay simple messages in a much shorter period by pointing to one picture. For example, in order to tell someone what is desired for breakfast, it might be more practical to quickly point to a picture that is readily accessible to the communicator, rather than to use an SGD to generate the message. In this case, the secondary communication system is the most effective and efficient method of communication.

How do you use a symbolic language system?

The techniques used to introduce and teach communication symbols play a significant role in why some users of symbolic communication become very successful while others are very poor. When individuals are non-verbal and have a language disorder, the techniques used for the introduction of symbols becomes even more important (Carlson 1997). First, determine which visual representation system the child understands and responds to most (objects, photographs, drawing, etc.; see Chapter 4), and in what contexts. The use of pictures as representative symbols is a much more complex skill and requires the individual to use the picture as a referent in various contexts (Stephenson and Linfoot 1996). Pictures may be used during activities such as sorting by category, using pictures to share information, or as a visual support to assist in structured comprehension tasks. These skills are required for efficient use of many AAC systems and SGDs. Many children who can identify and match pictures have difficulty using pictures for functional purposes. The following tips are practical strategies by Carlson (1997) for introducing symbols for communication and using them to enhance language skills.

Tip 1: Provide consistency within symbol categories or groups

Providing the same symbol to represent the same item is consistency. Consistency may also be thought of as how symbols are organized. When symbols are used for communication, they sometimes do not follow the rules of consistency. Consistency, however, may be achieved with the use of colors and locations. On communication boards, people are depicted on a yellow background and verbs are depicted on a green background. Some representations such as "yes," "no," "name," and "bathroom" are consistently placed in the same location throughout the pages of one symbolic system in order to make it easier to identify vocabulary on other systems when newly introduced (Carlson 1997).These shared common visual characteristics assist the child who uses symbolic representations to generalize meaning and use of a system. It is therefore important to be consistent when organizing systems and providing instruction.

Tip 2: Challenge "developing" language skills

Choose organizational strategies that will facilitate and enhance the development of expressive and receptive language skills. Symbolic materials should adhere to the activity procedure, grammatical structures, and semantic categories. Organizing and arranging the vocabulary according to the activity provides the child who is using the symbolic system with the appropriate vocabulary. Organizing and arranging the vocabulary in a symbolic language system according to the sentence structure may be done for sentence-based methods. A communication board organized from left to right with columns for *people* then *verb*, then *location* would provide a visual cue to sentence structure. The child could easily generate the message "I go store" with left-to-right progression as in speech. Finally, using categories to organize vocabulary can help the child understand language and how words fit into semantic categories.

Tip 3: Provide access to a large vocabulary set

In addition to the developmental educational vocabulary established for the child's age and cognitive levels, it is important to allow the child who will use the symbolic representation system to help select words and symbols to be placed on the system. Involving the child provides an excellent opportunity to gather vocabulary that is relevant and motivating. People in their lives, age appropriate vocabulary, social emotional requests (i.e. "Leave me alone", "I'm tired"), and vocabulary common to the child's culture and dialect are examples of vocabulary that may be important to the child. These messages are integrated with the academic and social vocabulary utilized in everyday educational and therapy activities providing personalization that is comfortable and gratifying for the child.

W
H
E
N

When do you use symbolic language systems?

Symbolic language systems are used when:

- vocabulary is predictable

- there is a reasonable limit to the number of vocabulary or messages needed

- it is an easier, faster method to generate desired messages.

Symbolic language systems are flexible, and individualized communication systems are customized to the particular communicative needs of the child. They may be used when the child consistently engages in activities on a regular basis (e.g. lunch, free-time choices, circle time). The flexibility that many symbolic language systems offer allows for multiple uses of the systems during varied communicative settings.

Predictable vocabulary

Symbolic language systems are used in communicative settings that offer predictable, static vocabulary. There should be reasonable limitations in the number of vocabulary options that may be expressed. An example of this is a restaurant topic page where menu items are listed or pictured and the child's desired choices may be readily accessed.

Figure 3.1 depicts an example of a fast-food menu that may be used for ordering. This menu page may be used specifically for instances when a child is going to a fast-food restaurant while at school or with a family. Using this page makes it easier to communicate the order. It is faster to generate the message, easy to carry, and requires less effort to relay the message. The available vocabulary is limited to the communicative needs for this occasion.

Classroom group activities (e.g. morning circle, weather, activity requests, and counting activities) that require a predictable finite number of vocabulary options is another example of a communicative setting that would be appropriate for a symbolic language system.

Figure 3.1 Fast-food menu

Figure 3.2 depicts the types of pages that may be included in a communication binder during a morning circle group activity. The binder contains multiple pages. Each page is topic-specific, containing vocabulary that relays messages within that topic.

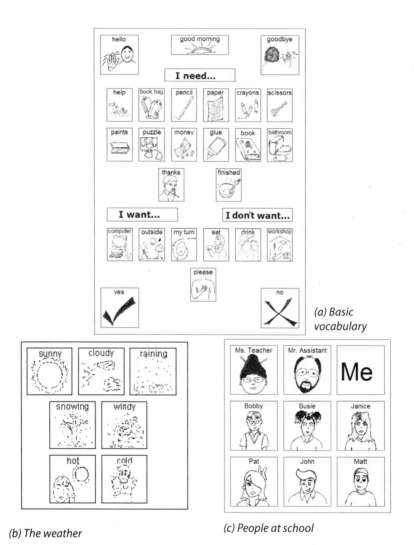

(a) Basic vocabulary

(b) The weather

(c) People at school

Figure 3.2 Sample pages for a communication binder

Limitations in vocabulary

Symbolic language systems are used when there are limitations in communicative or vocabulary needs. A symbolic language system may sufficiently accommodate the communicative needs of individuals who have limited language capacity or communicative needs. Due to limitations in the number of pictures that may be included in symbolic systems, the most desired or needed vocabulary is selected. Figure 3.3 is an example of an eye gaze chart that may be used by children to relay basic wants and needs, especially when physical limitations prohibit the use of symbolic language systems that require the ability to point or turn pages.

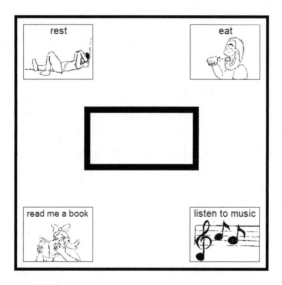

Figure 3.3 An eye gaze chart

Alternative communication methods

There are circumstances that make using a symbolic language system a more efficient method of communication. This is the case when symbolic language systems are used as a secondary method of communication. They are often used with the child who has an SGD as the primary method of communication. When the device is not operational and in need of repair or merely unavailable, expressive communication may be supplemented using a symbolic language system. This system will not offer the same message capacity; however, basic wants and needs can be relayed effectively.

There are also circumstances when the use of symbolic language systems may be more time efficient to use. For example, the time it would take to start an electronic device and complete the multiple sequences necessary to generate a message would be significantly longer than using a fast-food restaurant page where items to be ordered are included and the user can point to desired items. It is also easier for children to use a TV show and channel page, which includes their favorites, than for them to use an SGD to communicate their requests to their parents.

Symbolic language systems may also be used when the primary SGD cannot be easily managed in a particular setting. At times, symbolic language systems are taken on shopping trips or quick trips in the community because they are portable and easily accessible.

Finally, symbolic language systems are used when the communication partner has difficulty understanding or interpreting the desired message. Communication breakdowns might occur when the individual is using sign language, gestures, or vocal approximations. The partner needs specific training or prior experience with the communicator to interpret these messages. Symbolic language systems often do not require prior training or knowledge to interpret accurately.

Symbolic language systems are used when relaying concrete and predictable messages. They may be applied to any communicative environment throughout the school day and at home.

Figures 3.4–3.7 are examples of vocabulary that may be used in symbolic language systems for various communicative situations.

Symbolic language systems are generally not optimal when:

- the communicative needs of the child surpass the vocabulary capacity of the systems

- the communicator is in an environment in which new messages are needed.

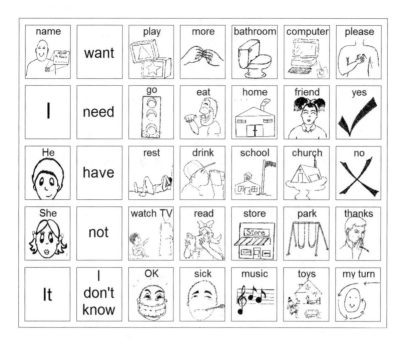

name	want	play	more	bathroom	computer	please
I	need	go	eat	home	friend	yes
He	have	rest	drink	school	church	no
She	not	watch TV	read	store	park	thanks
It	I don't know	OK	sick	music	toys	my turn

Figure 3.4 A communication board

Personal Information

Name _____

Address _____

City _____
State _____ Zip ____

Phone _____

Birthdate _____

Figure 3.5a Personal information page

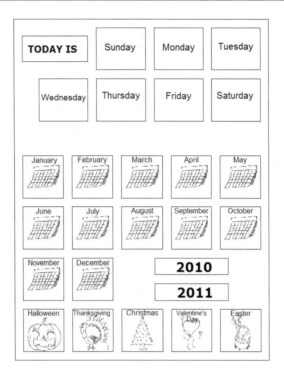

Figure 3.5b Calendar words

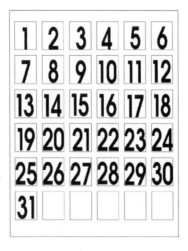

Figure 3.5c Dates in the month

Figure 3.6 I am feeling…

*Figure 3.7 Activities

W
H
E
R
E

Where can you get help?

Carlson, F. (1997) *Creating Communication Displays.* Unity, ME: Poppin and Co.

Stephenson, J. and Linfoot, K. (1996) "Pictures as Communication Symbols for Students with Severe Intellectual Disability." *Augmentative and Alternative Communication 4*, 244–255.

PART II

Strategies to Support Learning

Part II of *Rising to New Heights* provides a wealth of information to assist individuals facing the unique challenges of addressing the needs of children who do not respond to the typical techniques and strategies for learning. Children with ASD and significant developmental delays often fall into this category. The limited ability to address the specific needs of these children may lead to an environment for the educator that is disruptive, chaotic, unsuccessful, and at times combative. It is no wonder that the reality of working with these children strikes a cord of fear, at least to some degree, in individuals who are presented with the challenge of teaching this population.

It often appears that fear is precipitated by a sheer lack of understanding. Educators, therapists, and parents ask why children behave in a certain manner, and what can be done to help them? Ironically, teachers' fears and lack of understanding are often identical to those of the children they are charged to teach. In Part II, readers will learn that many of the behaviors displayed by a child with autism or other pervasive developmental disabilities are prompted by the inability to clearly answer the following questions:

- Where do I need to be?
- What do I need to do?
- How much do I need to do?
- What comes next?

The inability to answer these same questions creates anxiety and avoidance for educators, therapists, and parents when presented with the challenge of working with these children. Strategies are provided in Part II in an attempt to assist the interventionists in answering the questions, and to equip them with enough information to help children answer the above questions. Visual strategies and social stories give added information and tools to allow children to comprehend the instructions and communication of others. This added information supports the interventionists' efforts to address the specific needs of the child. Part II provides strategies to support learning by considering the individual learning styles of the child. Interventions are offered, with information detailing *Who* would benefit; *What* is entailed; *Why*, *How* and *When* the strategies should be used; and *Where* to get further help.

We have written Part II with the intent that readers will:

- understand and overcome their initial fear when working with children with ASD or other developmental disabilities who are not responsive to typical teaching strategies

- develop a better understanding of the children and what prompts their behavior, language, and learning

- develop goals and implement strategies that address the specific learning patterns of children

- achieve consistent progress and success in individual goal attainment.

4 | VISUAL SUPPORTS

Who would benefit from visual supports?

A world full of words is frequently too overwhelming for many children to comprehend. For children with a PDD such as an ASD or a developmental disability accompanied by difficulty understanding auditory input, verbal instructions might cause confusion, anxiety, or seemingly non-compliant behavior. In our work with students or young children with PDD, multiple disabilities, orthopedic handicaps or emotional impairment, visual tools have supported the comprehension and expression of language. With similar findings, Hodgdon (2003), and Massey and Wheeler (2000) also reported that benefit from visual supports may be gained by individuals diagnosed with developmental delay, aphasia, dyslexia, behavior disorder, attention deficit disorder, language delay or disorder, and mental impairment, among other conditions.

To assist with understanding instructions and expectations, families, teachers, speech language pathologists, and other educators may employ visual strategies to support and improve a child's receptive language. Hodgdon (2003) proposed that by utilizing visually mediated communication (VMC), focus shifts to improvement of receptive abilities. Hodgdon contended that relying upon a collection of visual tools enhances a child's comprehension, participation, and, ultimately, expressive communication. While visual strategies have been shown to improve the involvement, participation, and comprehension of children with autism, the tools may be equally successful for those with other diagnoses as well.

What are visual supports?

There are a number of different types of visual strategies used to promote a child's success. In *Rising to New Heights*, we begin discussion of visual supports with an examination of *schedules*. Other visual strategies (to be presented subsequently) include mini-schedules, calendars, work systems, social stories, choice boards, task organizers, checklists, photos, and symbols. Each of these supports may be viewed by the child with autism, as may other naturally occurring supports such as facial expressions, gestures and body language, and various items in the environment that children can look at and learn how to interpret. The ability to look at the supports boosts the child's comprehension, especially when auditory difficulties exist, as in many children with autism or other disabilities that affect their ability to learn or communicate.

Schedules

A picture schedule is an example of a visual tool that offers information to children with autism or other challenges to learning and communication (Hodgdon 2003). Schedules may inform students of regular events that are to occur, new activities that might ensue, changes to the normal routine, the sequence of daily activities, or when an activity is to happen or end (Hodgdon 2003, PaTTAN 2006).

Whether in object, photographic, symbolic, or written form, schedules have the potential to provide structure to both classroom and home routines. Schedules help clarify verbal instructions, aid children in organizing and predicting activities, and may motivate them to complete tasks when notified of upcoming transitions or reinforcing activities (TEACCH 2006).

Schedules may be constructed for home implementation, general classroom use, customized for individual use, or created to visually represent steps within a routine (a mini-schedule). In the schedule shown in Figure 4.1, the vertical schedule instructs the child on each phase of the mealtime routine, in which two additional mini-schedules are embedded. First, the hand-washing routine illustrates the sequence of steps necessary to wash hands appropriately. Similarly, the second mini-schedule shows the steps children are to take when getting their food. Mini-schedules break down the sequence of steps for an activity that is difficult for the child to complete independently. By segmenting the task into smaller steps, it is easier for children to engage successfully in the routine. Figure 4.2 on p. 68 shows a FIRST/THEN mini-schedule, while Figure 4.3 shows a similar NOW/NEXT tool (D'Amore 2005). The mini-schedules in Figure 4.4 on p. 69 present children with a reward system, indicating that IF they do as requested THEN they will be rewarded with a desirable item or activity.

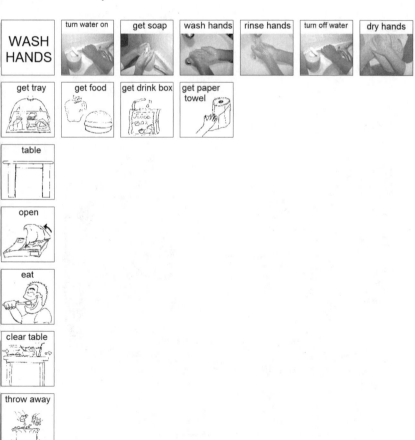

Figure 4.1 Mealtime, with two mini-schedules

FIRST

reading

FIRST

computer

THEN

math

THEN

workshop

(a)   *(b)*

Figure 4.2 "FIRST/THEN" boards

Figure 4.3 "NOW/NEXT" board

IF

breakfast

THEN

paint

Figure 4.4 "IF/THEN" board

Tool time: putting other visual supports to work

A variety of additional materials may be utilized to lend visual support to improve a child's communication, behavior, learning, and social interactions. Calendars are a familiar tool for both classroom and home. At school, a calendar can inform the child not only of regular activities and events, but also of changes to the normal schedule, thereby preparing the child and accommodating unexpected occurrences. Figure 4.5a on p. 71 shows a home schedule, while Figure 4.5b shows one that can be created and applied at school. Calendars (Figure 4.6 on p. 71) are valuable organizational tools that provide information, while helping children comprehend time and events.

Family or educational team members may improve a child's ability to comprehend and express language, with a choice board. A choice board informs children of the items from which they may choose. A board may be constructed to easily and readily depict choices in an array of settings, such as mealtime at home, school, or a restaurant; materials to select in a work station; or rewards for good behavior with a babysitter. Choices may be represented by actual or miniature objects, photographs, line drawings, or other media readily understood by the user. A child, who typically becomes frustrated by an inability to communicate preferences, may be assisted to do so via a choice board.

Bloomfield (2005) has created several teaching tools designed to clarify information effectively for students with autism or other special learning needs. The "Fold-up" is a portable material that groups six supports into one handy tool, applicable across various environments. One component of Bloomfield's "Fold-up" is the "Wait card" that helps children understand they must temporarily stop an activity they can return to later. The "Wait card" is also useful in instructing that it is not time for a particular task or event – that the child must *wait* until the card is removed, before initiating the activity. The "Count down card" informs children how much longer an activity will last and is useful in assisting them to transition to the next routine or activity. In a different approach, Bloomfield applies the "Bumper sticker" as a reminder of positive, desirable behavior. Symbols represent what the child is to do, rather than reiterating typical classroom "Don't rules". We have created similar supports, which visually remind students of what they are to do or where they are to be. Our "Reminder strips" may be mounted to a student's desk or carried in a wallet when in the community. Our symbolic directives may be bound in a "Flip book" worn around an adult's neck. The adult first teaches the children how the tool is used, and then, when they experience difficulty with compliance or comprehension of instructions, they are shown a symbol depicting the target behavior, in a more positive approach. Figure 4.7 on p. 72 illustrates Bloomfield's "Fold-up" visual support.

(a) Getting ready for school

(b) Arrival at school

Figure 4.5 Morning routines

Sunday	Monday	Tuesday	Wednesday	Thursday	Friday	**Saturday**
			1 School, Doctor	2 School Return books	3 School	4 No school, Visit Nana
5 Church	6 School Gym clothes	7 No school, Conferences	8 School Zoo trip, $$	9 School Return books	10 School Sissy home	11 No school

(a) Home

Sunday	Monday	Tuesday	Wednesday	Thursday	Friday	Saturday
			1	2 Library	3 Art	4 No school
5 No school	6 Phys Ed	7 Music	8 Zoo trip	9 Library	10 Art	11 No school

(b) Classroom

Figure 4.6 Calendars

(a) Waiting, visual directives   *(b) Count down*

Figure 4.7 Visual reminders for improving behaviour

Why use visual supports?

It is critical for a student with autism or other disabilities to know what is expected in the daily routine, and what comes next. When such information is lacking, behavior problems may occur, along with difficulty with organization and transitioning between activities (Rogers and DeFoore 2004). Wheeler and Carter (1998) and Hodgdon (2003) agree that behavioral problems in children with autism often stem from poor communication skills. Visual supports help bridge the gap, by facilitating comprehension, thus assisting children with learning difficulties to understand the myriad of demands placed upon them better, and consequently, decreasing behavior problems.

Schedules, one type of visual support, are an effective method of helping children function more independently and increase their on-task behavior (Bopp *et al.* 2004, Massey and Wheeler 2000, Zimbelman *et al.* 2006). According to Bopp *et al.*, use of visual schedules by children with autism has been associated with a decrease in disruptive behavior, aggression, tantrums, and property destruction. In older children, use of visual schedules enhances learning and improves the ability to perform daily living tasks (Bopp *et al.* 2004; Kimball *et al.* 2003, Wheeler and Carter 1998, Zimbelman *et al.* 2006). Independent use of visual schedules permits some children with learning or behavior problems to demonstrate appropriate on-task behavior and self-management skills.

For many children, verbal instructions may come and go too quickly for them to grasp. Visual supports give added information and tools to allow children to, comprehend the instructions and communication of others. Because children with autism typically demonstrate auditory processing deficits (Edelson 2007), they, and those displaying other disabilities, are at a disadvantage in a world-of-words they do not understand. The outcome is frequently apparent non-compliance, disruption, tantrums, emotional melt-downs, or off-task behavior.

Edelson (2007) suggests children with autism and those with auditory processing deficits may hear speech sounds, but not perceive their meaning. Teachers, families, and others may misinterpret the lack of speech comprehension as an unwillingness to comply. Visual strategies in general, and schedules in particular, supply the tools necessary to build an effective method of presenting information to children who cannot rely upon comprehension of the spoken word alone. The visual tools create an atmosphere of understanding, awareness of expectations, and an environment of familiarity, success, and high functioning, whether at home, in school, or in the community. Such a learning environment, conducive to comprehension and success, is possible because visual cues provide the structure students require in order to participate effectively and avoid behavior problems.

While auditory skills might be affected adversely by a PDD, through implementation of visual strategies, a platform for enhanced communication, behavior, and learning is built. Primary reasons for using visual tools then, according to Hodgdon (2003), are to (a) improve language comprehension and expression, (b) give information, (c) offer support throughout life routines, (d) teach skills, (e) prevent problems, and (f) intercede when a problem occurs. While these are explicit advantages for children, adults in their world may also benefit from the use of visual tools. The overwhelming fear factor may be dissipated through the understanding and completion of strategies that improve a child's comprehension, expression, behavior, and social interactions. The intention of this guide is to assist families and interventionists in equipping children with the tools needed to succeed.

How do you develop a visual support system?

A daily schedule is designed to represent visually the activities to be conducted throughout the day. The schedule may be a general one, depicting the sequence of classroom events, or a specific one developed for an individual student or activity.

Each visual schedule system must be unique to the student for whom it is intended, or to the classroom where it will be applied. It will be helpful to take the following factors into consideration when developing a visual schedule system:

Important factors to consider when developing visual supports

- Student's interests, strengths, and abilities.
- Collaboration among team members (families, teachers, assistant, speech-language pathologist, occupational therapist, other interventionists).
- Team's acceptance of and commitment to using visual supports.
- Team's understanding of and training in visual supports and schedules.
- Team's consistent use of schedules.
- Physical structure and organization of room (see Chapter 6).
- Consistent location of schedule.

- Student's comprehension and recognition of objects, photographs, line drawings, icons, or words.

- Visual schedule representation obvious to the student.

- Availability of the tools required to successfully complete the activity.

- Carryover use of schedules from school and home to other settings (Kamp and McErlean 2000; Wheeler and Carter 1998).

Selecting schedule representations: what to use?

The selection of visual representations might follow a hierarchy such as this, shown in Figure 4.8 on p.76:

- Real objects.

- Miniature real objects.

- True object-based icons (drawing, photograph, box remnant) cut into actual shape or outline of the item.

- Photographs.

- Detailed drawings.

- Line drawings.

- Written words (Wisconsin Assistive Technology Initiative 2000).

For young children, or those at a very concrete receptive language stage, it may be best to begin by introducing real objects. Small or doll's house toys may be used to represent a number of activities in a child's day. For instance, a doll's chair may depict that it is time to sit at the table or work station to complete a task. A spoon may be used for mealtime, or a miniature tennis shoe may be carried as the child walks to the gym. Choose an item that is easily recognized by the child and associated with the routine.

Once created, the schedule must become a consistent part of the child's daily routine. Whether developed for use at home or school, the family, teacher, or other interventionist is to begin the day by discussing with the child the upcoming events and the accompanying expectations. An aligned strategy, which also visually supports the

(a) Real objects

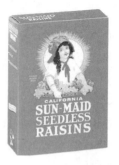

(b) Miniature real objects

(c) Photograph

(d) Container remnant

raisins

(e) Detailed drawing

(f) Written words

Figure 4.8 Hierarchy of visual representations

child in understanding upcoming events, is the social story, discussed in Chapter 5. Adults might find social stories an effective method of further preparing children for specific events, particularly those which are problematic for them.

When first introducing a schedule or mini-schedule, the adult is to model the expected behavior. In this manner, the child is more likely to learn not only the sequence of events, but also exactly how the tasks are to be completed. The adult examples of appropriate behavior may be withdrawn gradually, until the child is able to complete the routines independently (Kimball *et al.* 2003). Again, it is important to *teach* children how to perform and behave, then provide visual supports so they will do so successfully and independently. By supporting children's receptive language and understanding of events, improvement should occur in expressive language as well.

"Musts" for creating schedules

Developing an effective visual support system is a time-consuming endeavor; therefore, you must plan for the success of its implementation. By following the suggestions appearing later, adults will assist children in predicting and comprehending their activities, thus eliminating an element of fear from their lives. A number of decisions must be reached during the process of developing a visual support system. Here, we share what we believe you must do, must avoid, and must have in order to create and implement effective visual strategies.

MUST DO
Team up!

Elicit commitment and input from all team members (e.g parents, teachers, paraprofessionals, speech-language pathologists, occupational therapists, other interventionists)

Get organized!
Plan for use of the support.
Who's who?

- Who will create the support?
- Who is the intended user (adult or child)?

What's what?

- What is the intended purpose of the support?
- What is the expected outcome (e.g. improved comprehension, expression, behavior, transitions)?

When's the best time?

- Review the daily schedule of activities.
- Decide when the support is required.

Do be choosy!

Select type of representation (e.g. objects, photographs, drawings, words), size, and color.

Where in the world?

Where will the support be located (e.g. home or school, specific classroom or location, during transitions)?

Semi-permanent, movable, or portable?

All aboard!

Train all members on appropriate use of the support.

Get set! Go!

Create the system, after considering the "Must do" list and gathering the "Must haves".

Introduce system to the child.

Engage in trial runs.

Modify as necessary.

MUST NOT DO

Fail to teach the child to use the supports.

Give up if the system does not appear to work immediately.

Overlook the child's interests, abilities, skills, and preferences.

Use supports that are cluttered; instead, use clear, concise representations.

Be inconsistent with the use of the system.

Neglect to continuously collaborate and communicate with other team members, especially families.

MUST HAVE

Appropriate objects, remnants, cut-outs, and other picture sources.

Digital images (e.g. internet search, graphic software clipart, photo CD)

Line drawings.

Digital camera.

Computer and printer.

Laminator, sheet protectors, and sheet self-stick laminate.

Poster board, sentence strips, and card stock.

Velcro®, magnets, paper clips, hooks, metal rings, and lanyard.

Determination to provide the necessary support to allow children to succeed.

Motivation to overcome the fear factor.

Flexibility, willingness to change, listen, share, and learn from others.

When is it appropriate to use visual strategies?

It is appropriate to implement visual schedules when educating or providing interventions for students with PDD, multiple disabilities, orthopedic handicaps, or emotional impairment, or young children. It is essential to offer visual supports when students need strategies to help them prepare for and organize their day, as well as to anticipate changes and transitions that might occur. As stated earlier in this chapter, we contend that visual supports are useful when seeking to improve language skills, behavior problems, social skills, and ability to learn.

The type of schedule created (objects, photographic, drawings, symbols, or word-based) is dependent upon the needs and abilities of the children involved.

Figure 4.8 shows a hierarchy of visual representations one might use when selecting the representation that best matches a child's abilities. (Wisconsin Assistive Technology Initiative)

Introducing visual strategies?

When first introducing a visual schedule to a young non-reader with autism and language delays, a teacher might begin by using real objects. A spoon might represent lunch, whereas a marker might be used with a young girl who is a visual learner. She would remove the marker from the schedule and carry it as she walks to the Art Room. The support not only signals what is next, but it is also useful in the transition from one room to the next, by serving as a reminder of what is to come. For children who understand icons, the object (marker, in our example) might be replaced with a symbol for art, along with the printed word to support literacy skills. This approach would be applicable to students in the class who comprehend that the symbol represents art class.

Introducing different types of visual supports

Figure 4.9 illustrates four possible types of schedules, using real objects, photographs, line drawings, or words. The strategy selected will be decided based upon the needs and abilities of the students.

A checklist (Figure 4.10) might be used when employing visual schedules with children who are readers. With modeling and repetition, children become independent in their ability to refer to and check-off the activities of the day, as they are completed. They review the schedule to determine what is coming next. Initially, it may be helpful to begin with separate morning and afternoon schedules.

When developing a visual schedule, in order to keep an introductory support system manageable, it is advisable to begin first with the major events of the day. The teacher, family member, or

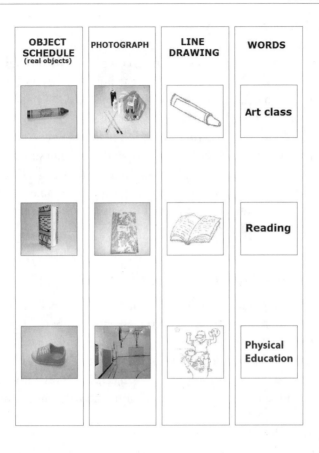

OBJECT SCHEDULE (real objects)	PHOTOGRAPH	LINE DRAWING	WORDS
			Art class
			Reading
			Physical Education

Figure 4.9 Four types of visual schedules

Time	Activity	Completed
9:00	Arrive/Breakfast	√
9:30	Occupational therapy	√
10:00	Reading	√
10:30	Art	
11:00	Speech therapy	
11:30	Work station	
12:00	Lunch	

Figure 4.10 Checklist schedule

other adult models how to engage in tasks and activities depicted by the schedule, and how to indicate their completion.

Indication of completion may be accomplished by turning over a symbol that has been clipped to the schedule. Alternately, a symbol or object that has been attached with Velcro® may be removed and placed in a "FINISHED" envelope or container.

As children learn the routine of following the schedule, many eventually become able to manage it without adult intervention. Ability to adhere to the schedule independently is a goal of visual support use. As discussed previously, positive outcomes of visual strategies may include improved comprehension, expression, behavior, and learning opportunities.

Using mini-schedules

When including the major routines of the day is not enough for children who require increased structure and support, then mini-schedules may be utilized.

One type of schedule that belongs in this category is a "FIRST/THEN" board. Using pictures or small objects to represent what is to be done, children learn that *first* they must complete one action, *then* another one is to occur.

Figure 4.5a is a mini-schedule informing the child that the first activity will be reading group, followed by math work. Figure 4.5b is similar; however, this support assists the student with transitioning from the preferred routine of computer time to the next activity of going to the vocational workshop. This visual strategy informs the students of what they are to do and where they are to be now, while preparing them for what will happen next. As discussed previously, when the work or activity has been completed, the picture or object is to be placed in the FINISHED container.

D'Amore (2005) published a similar mini-schedule (Figure 4.3) that follows a "NOW/NEXT" hierarchy. This tool is most effective when used to display what the child is currently doing, and what comes next, thus lessening anxiety due to uncertainty and transitions.

A similar visual tool is the "IF/THEN" board. This support differs, however, in its use as a reward system. Families may use the board in Figure 4.4 to indicate that IF the child eats breakfast, THEN painting is next. Upon completion of the activity, pictures are put in the designated FINISHED location, keeping consistency and expectancy in the routine.

Mini-schedules are useful in targeting certain events or tasks in the daily schedule that a child has difficulty completing. It breaks a larger task into smaller steps that are easier for the child to handle.

As children begin their day, the use of schedules is to start at home. Families will likely find their morning activities proceed more smoothly when children are provided with a visual representation of each upcoming activity. The day gets off to a smooth start, which is then continued at school. In this manner, not only is the fear factor reduced in adults, but for children as well. In *Rising to New Heights*, we contend that visuals reduce children's anxiety regarding the unknown or resistance to change by preparing them with information and strategies to cope.

Figure 4.5a shows a mini-schedule of "Getting ready for school" routine, while Figure 4.5b illustrates the steps children take when arriving at school.

When visual strategies are utilized, whether a visual support of the "Arrival at school" routine, or a real object depicting the departure activities at the end of the school day, the unfolding of the day is anticipated and controlled. Continuity of expectations and control is paramount; therefore, there is never a time to abandon the use of schedules. Students' appropriate use indicates their understanding of the schedule and ability to gain from it, not that they have "learned" it and no longer need the support.

The importance of timing

One of the most important factors to consider regarding when to use visual schedules is to use them consistently. Not only are children expected to use schedules regularly to organize their activities, but adults must also take the initiative in making the supports a consistent part of classroom and home routines.

Just as important as consistency, an integral part of successful visual strategy use is allowing for change. It is crucial to allow for changes to the daily routine, and to prepare students in advance for their occurrence. Educators might not know well in advance when a change will arise; yet, they must be ready with a symbol or strategy to depict that something different will occur. This may consist of the universal sign Ⓞ indicating that a particular routine is cancelled for the day.

In Figure 4.5b on p. 71, an X has been placed over the work shop activity, meaning that it will not take place that day. A symbol for the alternate event would be posted instead. A clear plastic container lid, piece of laminate, or transparency could be used to draw the null symbol or X.

Using other types of visual strategies

As with using schedules, calendars may be implemented at school as well as at home. Calendars are discussed each night to inform the child of what will occur the following day. They are then reviewed the next morning, to reinforce upcoming events and inform of any changes, so the unfolding of the day is predictable. In this manner, protests, tantrums, and non-compliance are less likely to occur.

Calendars may be used to assist children in organizing their day. Figure 4.6 shows calendars that are used at home or at school, respectively. The tool supports children by preparing them for what is to occur, particularly for activities that depart from the normal routine. According to Bloomfield (2005), the best time to introduce visual strategies, such as her "Fold-up" support, is when adults want to assist children with transitioning smoothly or behaving appropriately. The Fold-up may be used across settings because it is easily portable. The display of symbols assists children, such as those with autism or other disabilities who have difficulty understanding verbal language. The tool promotes positive behavior, and through direct instruction the children learn the expected behavior. Bloomfield (2005) cautions that it is advisable to present the tool at the beginning stages of behavioral difficulties, rather than when an incident has escalated.

It is important to customize visual supports according to the needs of the child involved. Figure 4.7 shows components similar to those contained in Bloomfield's Fold-up—that is, Waiting, Visual directives and Counting down. However, educators or families who construct a similar tool would base it upon the individual needs of the child. One child might need a visual reminder to *wait*, while another might be better supported by a visual cue to *line up* at the appropriate time.

When deciding to use visual strategies, take these factors into consideration

- Child's comprehension level.

- Type of representation.

- Consistent use of strategy.

- Method of indication that routine has ended.

- Child's knowledge of what to do next.

- Provisions for change.

Where can you get help?

Bloomfield, B. (2005) Available at www.icontalk.com/downloads/Directions.pdf, accessed on 26 June 2009.

Bopp, K.D., Brown, K. and Mirenda, P. (2004). "Speech-language pathologists' roles in the delivery of positive behavior support for individuals with developmental disabilities." *American Journal of Speech-Language Pathology 13*, 1, 5–19.

D'Amore, D. (2005) Available at www.SpeechPage.com, accessed on 26 June 2009.

Edelson, S.M. (2007) *Auditory Processing Problems in Autism.* San Diego, CA: Autism Research Institute.

Hodgdon, L. (2003) *Visual Strategies for Improving Communication.* Troy, MI: QuirkRoberts Publishing.

Kamp, L. and McErlean, T. (2000) Available at www.setbc.org/download/Public/VSS.pdf, accessed 15 June 2009.

Kimball, J.W., Kinney, E.M., Taylor, B.A. and Stromer, R. (2003) "Lights, camera, action! Using engaging computer-cued activity schedules." *Teaching Exceptional Children 36*, 40–45.

Massey, N.G. and J.J. Wheeler (2000) "Acquisition and generalization of activity schedules and their effects on task engagement in a young child with autism in an inclusive pre-school classroom." *Education and Training in Mental Retardation and Developmental Disabilities 35*, 3, 326–335.

W
H
E
R
E

85

PaTTAN (Pennsylvania Training and Technical Assistance Network) (2006) Pennsylvania Department of Education. *Visual Strategies.* Available at www. pattan.net/files/instruction/visualstrat.pdf, accessed on 26 June 2009.

Rogers, L. and DeFoore, P. (2004) "How the HighScope approach supports children with autism spectrum disorders: visual strategies." *HighScope ReSource 23,* 1, 1–4.

TEACCH (2006) *Structural Teaching: TEACCH Staff.* Available at www.teacch.com/ educational-approaches/structured-teaching-teacch-staff, accessed 26 June 2009.

Wheeler, J.J. and Carter S.L. (1998) "Using visual cues in the classroom for learners with autism as a method for promoting positive behavior." *B.C. Journal of Special Education 21,* 3, 64–73.

Wisconsin Assistive Technology Initiative (2000) *Assistive Technology Tools and Strategies Assessment Manual for Children with Autism Spectrum Disorder.* Oshkosh, WI: Polk Library.

Zimbelman, M., Paschal, A., Hawley, S.R., Molgaard, C.A. and St. Romain, T. (2006) "Addressing physical inactivity among developmentally disabled students through visual schedules and social stories." *Research in Developmental Disabilities 28,* 4, 386–396.

5 | SOCIAL STORIES™

Who would benefit from Social Stories?

Social Stories were developed by Carol Gray, President of the Gray Center. They are intended for children who display incompetence during social situations. It is for those children who find some typical daily activities such as transitioning, turn taking, and playtime difficult and confusing. The child who would benefit from the use of Social Stories often has inappropriate, inaccurate, and offensive responses during social situations. This book, *Rising to New Heights*, identifies individuals who may benefit from Social Stories in order to alleviate or reduce negative, unexpected, unpredictable, disruptive, or repulsive behaviors resulting in dislike and fear of working with the student.

What is a Social Story?

A Social Story is a relatively short, detailed, written description of social situations specifically highlighting what a child is to expect from a situation and what is expected of the child. Social Stories provide children with accurate information about those situations that they may find difficult or confusing. The situation is described in detail and focus is given to a few key points: the important social cues, the events and reactions the children might expect to occur in the situation, the actions, and reactions that might be expected of them and why (Wallin 2004).

W H Y | Why use a Social Story?

Wallin (2004) describes many of the benefits of using Social Stories. They help children understand a social situation, reduce their anxiety when encountering a situation, and suggest appropriate responses for the social situation in question. They provide children with realistic insight and perspective on what is happening, and help them better understand, predict, and respond to the actions of others in the situation. Social Stories also provide information on social situations in a structured and consistent manner. This lends itself perfectly to the learning styles of individuals with autism, particularly when dealing with the abstract spontaneous skills and behaviors that occur in social interactions. Social Stories also teach social information through pictures and text, as opposed to speech or observation, which are notable areas of weakness for individuals with autism. Finally, Social Stories create a stress-free environment in which to teach appropriate behaviors in a social situation that may be difficult for the student, thereby creating the opportunity to practice with much less anxiety.

H O W | How do you write a Social Story?

In this chapter, techniques and procedures for writing Social Stories are described that will assist in intercepting the anxieties often experienced when addressing the challenges of students with social and behavioral difficulties. The first step in writing a Social Story is to identify the social situations in which a child displays inappropriate behaviors and responses, and then to choose one to focus on. The writing of the story can now begin. Social Stories are usually written in the first person and present tense. Each should provide enough information about a social situation to equip a child with the knowledge needed to be prepared and respond appropriately when such situations are encountered. There are four types of sentences used to present this information in a Social Story (Gray 2000):

1. Descriptive sentences provide detailed information about where the situation happens, who is involved, what is being done, and why it is being done. Example: When I am in the lunchroom, it sometimes gets very noisy because there are a lot of kids in there and they are all talking at the same time.

2. Perspective sentences give insight into the thoughts of those involved in a story; they provide details about what others are feeling and thinking. Example: The children are all talking because it is their free time and they like talking to their friends.

3. Directive sentences provide suggestions of appropriate responses specific to a child's needs. Example: When I hear all the noise, I know that there is not a problem and I can ignore it.

4. Control sentences are created by children as a "catch phrase" to help remind them of what has been learned; they help them remember a story or deal with a situation. They are not used often and only with high-functioning children. Example: Lunchroom noise is okay.

According to Carol Gray (2000), the recommended formula for writing Social Stories is to use five descriptive sentences for each directive sentence, which may include perspective sentences. Studies have indicated that Stories following this ratio are most effective.

When writing your Story, it is important to be mindful of the child's cognitive and maturity levels by using appropriate vocabulary and type size. Each Social Story should reflect the type and level of other literature the child may be encountering at home and at school. A kindergarten Story may consist of a single idea per page, with illustrations. A middle-school student might have a much longer Story, with more text and smaller font size. Figures 5.1–5.4 in illustrate sample Social Stories for different age groups. It is also important to remember that Social Stories are not merely to list desired or expected behaviors; rather, they are descriptions of social situations which helps children to understand social situations, thereby encouraging their ability to develop or learn appropriate positive interactions. It is therefore recommended to avoid the use of sentences that are inflexible and stated as a "command". Replace phrases like "I can" and "I will" with "I will try" or "I will work on" in directive sentences. "Usually" and "sometimes" should be used instead of "always," in perspective and descriptive sentences. An appropriate sentence for when disruptive behavior occurs after a visitor knocks on the door may be "I will try to remain calm and not run outside". As children become more successful with social stories, directive sentences may be eliminated making it the children's responsibility to develop behavioral responses that work best for them—the ultimate goal of Social Stories.

While text on paper is probably the easiest presentation to prepare and use, it may not be the most appropriate for every child, such as a non-reader. There are, however, a variety of presentation styles and options, such as those shown here, which may be used to meet the individual needs of children (Wallin 2004).

Illustrations

A child is provided with illustrations or photographs on each page depicting social situations and adding interest and visual cues about the intended message. It is important to use images that are simple, in order to ensure that a child with autism focuses on the intended image and not the background.

Symbols

The text of a Story may be supplemented with pictures representing any of the words or ideas in the Story. A true object-based icon, such as a cereal box label, may be used. A detailed drawing, a line drawing, or symbols generated from computer software such as Boardmaker are additional options that may be used in Social Stories. For beginning readers, PECS symbols or simple line drawings may be used instead of text for words that are unknown. A complete idea may be represented by one large symbol on a particular page. Figure 5.1 is an example of a Social Story augmented with pictures included to assist in the comprehension of the text.

There are lots of fun things to do at *school*.	I like to *color*, play with *blocks*, and play with the *doll house*.
When there are too many kids in an area I want to play in, my teacher says I cannot play there right now.	When the teacher says I cannot play right now, I sometimes get *angry*.
I do not have to get angry because if I *wait* I will get a *turn* soon. There are other fun things I can do while I wait.	When I *wait*, my classmates can play too and they can have fun and this makes them happy.
Having fun with the toys at school makes me *happy*.	I will take turns when I play with *toys* at school.

Figure 5.1 Sample Social Story for a young child for school

Social Stories on tape

When given a cue to turn the page, a child may read the written Story along with an on tape audio recording of the text.

Video

A child is videotaped acting out the expected behaviors in a social situation. The text is captioned on a video and eventually faded. The information about expected or appropriate behaviors in social situations is eventually provided by text alone.

Story boxes

Understanding of information provided and interest in Social Stories may be enhanced by children role-playing the social scene with props like small toy figures. This method is particularly beneficial for non-readers.

Wallin (2004) recommends that Social Stories are introduced and implemented with monitoring and fading strategies. A Story should be used with others involved with the children on a daily basis at school and at home as a way of reinforcement. After becoming familiar with a Story, the children should then retell it to others using their most effective expressive method whether it is speech, a symbolic language system or an SGD. When consistent success is noted at retelling the Story, the educational staff or family can refer to it when the appropriate social situations arise. Finally, an ongoing evaluation process is essential to gauge the effectiveness of a strategy used. Use data collection methods to obtain objective measures of the occurrence of targeted behaviors over time.

When do you use Social Stories?

It is appropriate to use Social Stories for any situation a child finds difficult to manage for whatever reason. They can be written for situations as common as appropriate behavior when transitioning between classrooms. Stories may also be written for individual difficulties that are not as common but specific to a child, such as appropriate items to eat.

Social Stories are used when children need answers to questions or clarification of uncertainties they have about social situations (Wallin 2004). There are instances throughout time spent in school and at home that may warrant a Social Story to answer questions children have about situations in which they find themselves. During arrival time, a Social Story may be written to assist children with where to go after getting off the bus, what to do when they get to where they should be, how to respond, and what to do next. Addressing these questions through Social Stories offer children a sense of comfort and familiarity that helps prevent inappropriate, negative, or otherwise undesired responses. Figure 5.1 is an example of a Social Story that may be used at arrival time for a young child.

There is no wrong time to do a Social Story. Any time a behavior consistently garners a response that is not beneficial to a child's academic, socio-emotional, health or safety status, a Social Story may be used as intervention. Some examples of when Social Stories may be used at school are meal or snack time, bathroom time, group time, independent work time, free time, and dismissal. Some situations that Social Stories may be used at home for are morning routines, bedtime, welcoming known or unknown visitors, and eating out. These are merely a few examples of when Social Stories may be used. There are an infinite number of opportunities for different Stories because they are individualized to a child's unique needs. Boxes 5.1–5.3 are examples of Social Stories that may be used at home.

Going for walks

When I walk, I sometimes grab strangers' hands and go with them.

This makes my mom very upset because she says
it is not safe to do this.

When I see a stranger, I will say "Hi" and continue to
walk with my mom.

Box 5.1 Sample Social Story for home

Sharing with Mom and Dad

I have lots of fun things to play with!

I have toys.

I have a Walkman®.

I have lots of music I like to listen to too.

Sometimes Dad or Mom need to use one of my fun things
like a toy or an ipod.

This is okay.

These things are mine, but it is okay for Mom and Dad to borrow.

When Mom or Dad say, "Can I borrow this?" I can say, "Okay!"

Mom or Dad will take very good care of my things.

They love me and they respect my things.

I will try to say, "Okay" when Mom or Dad want to borrow my things.

This will make them very happy!

Maybe I can borrow something of Mom's or Dad's someday too!

Box 5.2 Sample Social Story for home

When I feel angry

Sometimes I feel angry.

All people feel angry at one time or another.

When I get angry I will find my teacher, Mommy, Daddy, or another adult.

When I find them I will try to use words to tell them that I am angry.

I can say "I'm angry!" or "That makes me mad!"

It is okay to use words when I feel angry.

They will talk to me about what happened and about how I feel.

This might help me to feel better.

Wherever I am I can try to find someone to talk to about how I feel.

Box 5.3 Sample Social Story for an older child for home

Where can you get help?

Gray, C. (2000) *The New Social Story Book.* Arlington TX: Future Horizons, Inc.
Wallin, J. (2004) *An Introduction to Social Stories.* Available at www.polyxo.com/socialstories/introduction.html, accessed on 3 August 2009.

W
H
E
R
E

6 | STRUCTURED ENVIRONMENTS

W H O ## Who would benefit from a structured physical environment?

Young children or individuals with developmental disabilities, ASDs, behavior problems, or any condition that adversely affects their ability to learn, may benefit from structured, organized classroom and home environments. Characteristics of such children include: (a) organizational and directionality problems; (b) an auditory processing disorder or sensitivity to auditory stimuli; (c) impairment of other senses, including visual, tactile, vestibular, olfactory, and proprioceptive; (d) receptive language deficits, demonstrated through challenges to comprehension of directions, expectations, and rules; (e) memory problems, particularly for locations, the sequential order of tasks, or the schedule of events; (f) signs of being distracted easily; or (g) rigidity in routines and rituals. Whether in the home or at school, setting the stage, by engineering the physical environment, is essential to providing exceptional needs children with successful learning and functional experiences. In this book we provide readers with specific ideas on structuring the environment in order to improve learning opportunities for children.

What is meant by a structured physical environment?

A classroom that is structured effectively is one that is well organized, in terms of physical arrangement and the use of developmentally appropriate practices, activities, and materials. A structured classroom affords optimal interaction and social climate, and is orderly, due to the use of visual supports and routines (Alter and Conroy 2005). A well-designed room has designated areas, with clear boundaries for particular tasks. Materials are easily accessible, so children will know where to find required items, and also where they personally are supposed to be in order to complete tasks and participate in activities (TEACCH 2006). Classrooms or areas within the home that are arranged in this manner help reduce the fear factor in children by providing predictability, structure, and organization. Interventionists and families also benefit from working or living in a space that is orderly and arranged for optimum functionality.

To organize a room most appropriately, families and teachers must take into account the individual needs and abilities of the children. Increased visual supports and structure may be required for lower functioning children or those with problematic behaviors. Conversely, older children or students whose disabilities have less impact on comprehension or behavior may not need as much structure. Figure 6.2 illustrates a classroom designed to meet the needs of students with autism or other exceptional needs.

Why structure the physical environment?

According to researchers, students' appropriate behaviors increase, and inappropriate behaviors are more likely to decrease, when the environment is designed effectively (Alter and Conroy 2005; TEACCH 2006). When incorporating visual strategies into the classroom or home, such supports increase children's comprehension, independent functioning, and on-task behavior. Displayed schedules, choice boards, and sequential task prompts are among the tools that frequently reduce apparent non-compliance, disruption, or tantrums because they provide children with information, communicate expectations, and offer predictability.

A room arranged with intention informs children where they are supposed to be and what they are to do. The establishment of work stations clearly delineates workspace, tasks, and expectations. Well-designed workstations will further instruct children as to what is to be completed when the current work is finished. Work systems assist learners in several ways. They help: (a) when children have difficulty with verbal directions and the steps of an activity; (b) by using an organized and structured approach to teaching specific skills; (c) through alleviation of the frustration of not knowing expectations; and (d) when children learn by using visual supports (Do2Learn n.d.).

H
O
W

How do you organize the environment?

We propose that the first step in organizing a classroom for children with exceptional needs is to consider the general environment. Location is key; therefore, ideally, a classroom for students with autism, for example, would be located near children of the same age. This would eliminate the stigma faced by an older child in a special education class located near much younger students. Having a bathroom nearby is an asset, especially if students are being toilet-trained or primed for independent movement for short distances throughout the school. For safety reasons, it is advisable to avoid classrooms with multiple exits, or exits to busy streets or external grounds, particularly if any of the students have a tendency to run away.

Children with autism and other exceptional needs frequently display dysfunctional sensory systems, necessitating consideration of their sensitivity to environmental stimulation. A child might be sensitive to light, especially fluorescent, requiring adjustment of the lighting. Sights might easily cause distractibility, as might particular sounds. A child might be tactile defensive and resistant to touch. The child's home and school teams must collaborate to determine a comprehensive sensory profile and modify the environment appropriately, while increasing the child's ability to adapt.

Room size is a crucial element in classroom organization, with a large room being preferable, allowing adequate space for workstations, centers, storage, screened areas, and optimal configurations. Size is also important when structuring a child's bedroom or play area at home. A small, cluttered space may interfere with sleep and attention to tasks, or may reduce opportunities for social interaction with family members and others in the home (TEACCH 2006). For children with sensory sensitivities, environmental factors such as lighting and noise levels must also be considered when determining location at home or at school. If not well planned, behavior problems may result, in response to over-stimulation, irritation, or distraction.

Once the space has been selected, the next step is to make specific arrangements within the room. Strategies for effectual organization may be based upon the basic configuration and subsequent modification of the room. Determine where work areas and stations are to be located within classrooms. For individual stations, the availability of a blank wall is an advantage because it reduces visual distractions. Desks and tables are faced toward the wall, helping the children focus on the work at hand. The height of furniture, chairs, sinks, and counters must be matched appropriately to the size of the children.

Portable dividers may be placed in the classroom to separate each child's space and work areas. Cabinets, bookcases, and shelving units may also be used to define specific areas and boundaries. Placing work areas near storage units facilitates independence, because the children are able to access required materials easily. The items required to complete a task are to be located where the work is done. For example, the table where puzzles are completed is located near the shelf where puzzles are stored. A literacy corner will be furnished with comfortable seating, including mats or beanbag chairs, and will have books of high interest on hand.

Placement of furniture in a housekeeping corner defines the boundaries, informs the children of what is expected to occur in that area, and indicates where objects are to be stored when finished. Additional methods of marking out a particular part of the room are by placing a carpet or a taped area on the floor. The use of labels is also helpful in structuring the environment. Labels can (a) indicate where materials belong, (b) identify children's work area, personal belongings, lockers or coat area, mailboxes, etc., and (c) improve language skills by showing the names of various objects in the room, around the school, or in the house (Hodgdon 2003). Labeling has the added advantage of increasing visual information to children, allowing them to access and replace materials in the proper location independently, and to understand where certain activities occur. With these supports, children with autism or other PDD are more likely to succeed in an environment that provides information giving meaning to locations, activities, and materials (Rogers and DeFoore 2004).

Another method of structuring the environment is to assign each child an individual symbol. John's symbol may be a yellow triangle, while Tamara's is a red square. When mounted properly, the symbols show John and Tamara where to sit, work, store their belongings, stand in line, or wait. An alternate strategy is to mount children's photographs to identify their areas.

To prevent behavior meltdowns (e.g. tantrums, crying, disruptive behavior), a designated area should be available where the child may take a break or choose a substitute activity, prior to a situation getting out of control. Parents are very astute at recognizing when meltdowns are about to occur. Increasing awareness of the triggers at home and describing them to school staff might help to reduce incidents of problem behavior and to rise above the disruption these cause both child and adult. With the assistance of the speech-language pathologist, the child will be given a method of communicating a desire to change activities, take a break, or move to a different space. Provision of choice boards (as described in Chapter 4) or photographs of various room stations and activities is an effective strategy for supplying children with a method of communicating their wants and needs.

These strategies are applicable to both home and school, although usually used in a smaller space at home. Environmental factors and room arrangement are equally important in each setting. In all settings, it is crucial to be able to monitor children; therefore, dividers and other boundary-setting furniture must be at a height where an adult is able to see the children at all times.

Using the TEACCH approach

The Treatment and Education of Autistic and related Communication Handicapped Children (TEACCH) approach, designed for those with autism spectrum disorder or communication deficits, places the individual at the core of its methods by focusing on the person's skills, interests, and needs (TEACCH 2006). Acknowledging a culture of autism, members of the TEACCH organization suggest that people with autism are part of a distinctive group with common characteristics (such as those described previously) who are different from, but not inferior, to others.

TEACCH (2006) recommends taking the following factors into consideration when arranging a child's environment:

- Is there adequate space for individual and group work?
- Are workstations available for students who require them?
- Are work areas in the least distractible settings?
- Are work areas marked so students can perform independently?
- Can the teacher visually monitor all work areas?
- Are there places for finished work?
- Are materials easily accessible and located near work areas?

Defining hallmarks of the TEACCH approach are provision of work stations, learning within a predictable work session, and use of a structured work system. TEACCH recommends work systems, like Shoebox Tasks®, that are simple and developmentally appropriate, with the potential for independent completion. Families and school staff establishing teaching and learning routines for children with autism will find such activities beneficial. Activities may be constructed with all required materials housed within a single container (e.g. basket, shoebox, or bag). Task requirements are visually clear, helping children organize their actions in order to complete tasks successfully and independently. In our experience, these activities are equally applicable for use with young learners and those with developmental disabilities, PDD, motor, auditory, or visual deficits. Inspired by commercially available task materials, teachers, therapists, and families have become very creative when fabricating their own activities to be completed during a structured work session. Whether purchased or custom-made, tasks must be clear, age- and ability-appropriate, motivating, and able to be completed independently, while under adult supervision.

Figure 6.1 presents a typical work station organized so children will easily know the answer to the following questions:

- How much work is there to do?

  Tasks are located to the child's left, within easy reach. The number of tasks (at the discretion of the adult) tells the child how much work there is to do.

- What is the work?

  The child knows what the work is by the visual structure of each task.

- When is the work finished?

  When all the tasks have been completed and placed in the finished basket, located to the child's right.

- What happens next?

  Directly after the child has finished working, there is a toy, treat, or indication of where to go next.

(TEACCH 2006)

Once the physical structure of the setting is well organized, families and school staff must also be aware of the interpersonal atmosphere, as well. Are adults attentive, patient, and caring? Do they reward appropriate behavior and provide assistance when necessary? The creation of a calm, comfortable environment, where caregivers and educators offer positive support, is expected to result in more appropriate behavior. As we stated earlier during our discussion on visual strategies, there is a need for consistency, in the physical environment, expectations, and interactions with adults. Setting the stage, by engineering the physical environment, assists children in overcoming the fear factor by providing them with predictability, routines, and expectations.

According to TEACCH (2006), the organization of the work environment and presentation of tasks answer the relevant questions in the following ways.

1. How much work is there to do?
   Tasks are located to the student's left, within easy reach. The number of tasks, as determined by the teacher, tells the student the amount of work to be completed.

2. What is the work?
   By the visual structure of each task, the student knows what the work is.

3. When is the work finished?
   Placement of all completed tasks in a FINISHED container, located to the student's right, indicates that the work is finished.

4. What happens next?
   Directly after the student has finished all tasks, a toy, treat, or signal of where to go indicates what to do next.

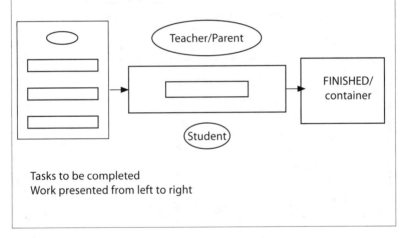

Tasks to be completed
Work presented from left to right

Figure 6.1 Structured TEACCH work session

When is it appropriate to structure the environment?

WHEN

The TEACCH approach is one method of structuring the environment effectively.

TEACCH is beneficial when children with autism or other exceptional needs are beginning to learn.

TEACCH strategies or similar approaches that organize the setting are to be applied when the child needs to know how much work there is to do, what the work is to be done, when the work will be finished, and what will happen next.

Figure 6.1 depicts a typical work station utilizing a left-to-right orientation, which clearly informs the child about the tasks to be completed.

Figure 6.2 illustrates a preschool classroom for children with disabilities. The room is clearly arranged into areas for working, playing, and eating. There are spaces for high-energy activities in the play area, as well as quiet reading or listening. Schedules, located throughout the classroom, provide visual support and predictability to the environment.

Each child is assigned a symbol, which is placed in several locations in the environment. Upon arrival, children locate their symbols in their cubbies. In the group area, each child sits on a chair or mat with the appropriate symbol. In the waiting area, when it is

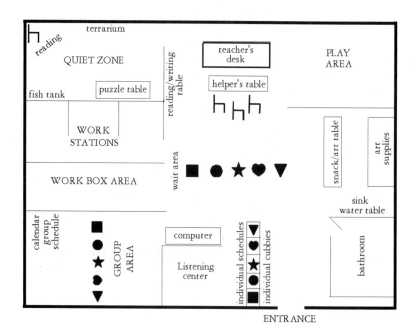

Figure 6.2 Structured classroom

time to transition to another room or activity, children know to wait on their individual symbol.

With such provisions, children, families, and interventionists are supported in their efforts to offer a setting conducive to learning. As noted previously, when equipped with adequate knowledge, families and educators are able to move past the fear factor some individuals experience when questioning how to structure a child's day, behavior, and surroundings.

Where can you get help?

Alter, P.J. and Conroy, M.A. (2005) "Environmental arrangements and visual supports to prevent problem behavior." Paper presented at the Addressing Challenging Behavior: The National Training Institute on Effective Practices Supporting Young Children's Social/Emotional Development conference, Clearwater Beach, Florida, May.

Do2Learn (n.d.) *Build a classroom.* Available at www.do2learn.com/organizationtools/classroom/buildaclassroom/index.htm, accessed on 3 August 2009.

Hodgon, L. (2003) *Visual Strategies for Improving Communication.* Troy, MI: QuirkRoberts Publishing.

Rogers, L. and DeFoore, P. (2004) "How the High/Scope approach supports children with autism spectrum disorders: visual strategies." *HighScope ReSource* 23, 1, 1–4.

TEACCH (2006) *Structures Teaching: TEACCH Staff.* Available at www.teacch.com/educational-approaches/structured-teaching-teacch-staff, accessed 26 June 2009.

W
H
E
R
E

PART III

Resources

The purpose of Part III is to provide basic introductory information on topics related to the themes presented in *Rising to New Heights*. Because the subjects may be of interest to families and school personnel, they are included here but not broadly enough to warrant full chapters. The following topics are discussed: sensory integration, applied behavior analysis, the Hanen Centre, routines, Chileda, and the S.U.C.C.E.S.S. Approach[SM], and national organizations that provide information on autism and other developmental disabilities are also listed.

7 | INFORMATION ON RELATED TOPICS

Sensory integration

Individuals with autism or other developmental disabilities may have a dysfunctional sensory system, with one or more of the senses being under- or over-reactive to stimulation (Hatch-Rasmussen 1995). According to Mailloux and Smith Roley (2001), sensory integration refers to neurological functioning, as well as to a specific theory and intervention approach emerging from the field of occupational therapy, propagated initially by Dr. A. Jean Ayres. Hatch-Rasmussen (1995) explained that sensory integration, an innate neurobiological process, refers to the brain's integration and interpretation of sensory stimulation from the environment. Sensory integrative dysfunction, conversely, is a disorder in which sensory input is not integrated or organized properly in the brain and may produce varying degrees of problems in development, information processing, and behavior.

A child with dysfunction within the tactile, vestibular, or proprioceptive systems may exhibit or fluctuate between the extremes of an overly high or low response to sensory input or activity level, or between constant motion and easy fatigue (Hatch-Rasmussen 1995). A normal tactile system sends information to the brain regarding touch, pain, temperature, and pressure, via nerves under the skin's surface. The vestibular system, within the inner ear, detects movement and changes in the position of the head, while the proprioceptive system refers to aspects of the muscles, joints, and tendons that provide one with awareness of body position (Hatch-Rasmussen 1995). When the three systems are dysfunctional, fine or gross motor coordination problems may be present, possibly resulting in speech and language delays or lowered academic performance. A child's sensory integrative dysfunction may also be exhibited through impulsivity, distractibility, lack of planning, or reacting to new situations with frustration, aggression, or withdrawal (Hatch-Rasmussen 1995).

Primarily utilized in pediatric treatment, interventionists employ sensory integration therapy to help a child with autism play like other children. The purpose of sensory integration therapy is to assist the child in (a) functioning more appropriately throughout daily activities by improving the ability of the brain to process sensory information, (b) inhibiting and modulating sensory information, and (c) processing a more organized response to sensory stimuli (Dempsey and Foreman 2001; Hatch-Rasmussen 1995).

Adapting to changes in the sensory characteristics of the environment poses challenges to children with autism or other developmental disabilities. Through assessment, occupational therapists or other interventionists analyze a child's engagement and participation in daily activities, from a sensory-integration perspective (Mailloux and Smith Roley 2001). Evaluation results indicate the sensory and motor underpinnings of the child's choices and capabilities while participating in daily life activities. Because children with autism have difficulties with cognition, language, attention, transitions, and social reciprocity, standardized tests are often an inappropriate method of determining sensory functioning (Mailloux and Smith Roley 2001). Rather, observations, in conjunction with family and teacher interviews, provide valuable information during assessment. Evaluation results lead interventionists to the goal of establishing or restoring a healthy lifestyle for children and their families by engaging the youngsters in meaningful occupations (Parham and Primeau 1997). According to Mailloux and Smith Roley, sensory integration therapy that seeks to achieve this goal is based upon the following framework:

- Use of a structured sensory environment that highlights the proprioceptive, vestibular, and tactile systems.
- A focus on tapping the inner drive of the child.

- Delivery of intervention in the context of play.
- "Artful vigilance" on the part of the therapist.
- Child-directed sessions.
- Elicitation of adaptive responses.
- Delivery of the "just right" level of challenge.
- Emphasis on active versus passive participation where the engagement in the activity is its own reward (Mailloux and Smith Roley 2001, p.117).

The Ohio Center for Autism and Low Incidence (OCALI) suggests families, educators, and interventionists may want to introduce the following supports to children with an ASD:

- Sensory integration activities.
- Sensory diet.
- Scheduled breaks for sensory activities.
- Desensitization strategies (ear plugs, iPod, shaping tolerance, etc.).
- Visual cueing strategy.
- Auditory integration therapy (AIT).
- Vestibular stimulation (such as swinging).
- Tactile stimulation (such as brushing parts of a child's body).
- Traditional occupational therapy.
- Environmental supports (workstations, waiting chairs, etc.).

Further information

American Occupational Therapy Association

4720 Montgomery Lane
PO Box 31220
Bethesda
MD 20824-1220
Tel: +1 (301) 652 2682
www.aota.org

Applied behavior analysis

Applied behavior analysis (ABA) is a systematic process of studying and modifying observable behavior through manipulation of the environment. ABA has been defined by numerous professionals in vastly different ways. Each interpretation of ABA tends to reflect the personal philosophies, experiences, and preferences of the individual. Saffran (2007) suggests that ABA is just as much about maintaining and using skills as it is about learning. According to Saffran, "applied" means practice, rather than research or philosophy. Behavior analysis may be read as learning theory—that is, understanding what leads to (or doesn't lead to) new skills. ABA principles are derived from extensive basic research, often with animals, but have realized popularity in applied therapy with autism and other developmental disorders. The process consists of an experimental approach to manipulating the environment and tracking alterations in behavior (Chiesa 1994).

Typically, most children learn basic language, socialization, and play skills through their daily activities, experiences, and observations. Children with autism learn much less from the environment. They are capable of learning, but it takes a very structured environment where conditions are optimized for acquiring the same skills that typically developing children learn naturally. ABA is a rule-governed approach for setting up the environment to facilitate learning (Saffran 2007). ABA therapy is used to teach behaviors to individuals with autism who may not otherwise acquire these behaviors spontaneously through imitation. ABA teaches these skills through use of behavioral observation and positive reinforcement or prompting to teach each step of a behavior (Simpson 2001). Generally, ABA involves intensive training of the therapists, extensive time spent in ABA therapy (20–40 hours per week), and weekly supervision by experienced clinical supervisors known as certified behavior analysts (Shook and Neisworth 2005).

Key aspects of the ABA process include:

- observing current behavior for topography (what the movement looks like), frequency, antecedents, and consequences

- breaking down desired skills into steps
- teaching the steps through repeated presentations of discrete trials
- tracking performance data to show changes over time (Autism Treatment Info 2005).

Discrete trial teaching

The most common and distinguishing type of intervention based on applied behavior analysis is discrete trial teaching. In discrete trial training, behaviors are segmented into basic functional units that are then presented, as explained by Wallin (2004). Wallin described the first step as involving teacher instruction. If a teacher thinks a child needs help responding correctly, he or she will provide a prompt, cue, or model to assist. Then, either with help or without, the child gives some response to the instruction. If the child responds incorrectly, the teacher provides further instruction and then gives the child another chance. If the child responds accurately, the teacher gives a reward or praise as encouragement. After the discrete trial is completed, the teacher pauses before continuing, to indicate that one step has been completed prior to continuing on to the next trial (Wallin 2004).

Saffran (2007) lists the following additional techniques commonly associated with ABA.

Chaining

The skill to be learned is broken down into small units for easy learning. For example, a person learning to brush teeth independently may start with learning to unscrew the toothpaste cap. Once this is learned, the next step may be squeezing the tube, and so on.

Prompting

The parent or therapist provides assistance to encourage the desired response from the student. Prompts are faded systematically and as quickly as possible from a more intrusive prompt to the least intrusive prompt, with completely independent responding as the goal.

Fading

The overall goal is for an individual, eventually, to not need prompts. This is why the least intrusive prompts are used, so the child does not become overly dependent on them when learning a new behavior or skill. Prompts are gradually faded out as new behavior is learned.

Generalization

Once a skill is learned in a controlled environment (usually during structured learning activities), it is taught in more general settings. Perhaps the skill will be taught in the natural environment. If the child has successfully mastered learning colors at the table, the teacher or parent may take the student around the house or school and then re-teach the skill in these natural environments.

Shaping

Shaping involves gradually modifying the existing behavior into the desired behavior. If a young boy engages with a dog by hitting it, he could have his behavior shaped by reinforcing interactions in which he touches the dog more gently. Over many interactions, successful shaping would replace the hitting behavior with patting or other gentler behavior.

Differential reinforcement

Reinforcement provides a response to the student's behavior that will most likely increase that behavior. It is "differential" because the level of reinforcement varies depending on the student's response. Difficult tasks may be reinforced heavily whereas easy tasks may be reinforced less heavily. Therapists must systematically change the reinforcement so that the student will eventually respond appropriately under natural schedules of reinforcement (occasional) with natural types of reinforcers (social).

Video modeling

One teaching technique found to be effective with some students, particularly young children, is the use of video modeling (the use of taped sequences as exemplars of behavior). It can be used by therapists to assist in the acquisition of both verbal and motor responses, and in some cases for long chains of behavior.

ABA has experienced its share of controversy over the years and has had many ethical challenges. Critics argue that it does not actually improve the skills of individuals with autism, but instead only teaches them to mimic neurotypical behavior without really understanding the meaning of the social cues they are using. Critics also argue that ABA teaches individuals with autism to suppress natural and harmless stimulatory behavior (stimming). Since the use of ABA has become widespread relatively recently, its long-term consequences and risks have not been studied. There have been claims that ABA is successful only because of the use of aversives that often cause post-traumatic stress disorder, anxiety, and clinical depression later in life (Dawson 2004). Dawson, a researcher, autism rights activist, and individual with autism, published an article challenging the ethical practices and claiming the scientific effectiveness of ABA.

The Hanen Centre

The Hanen Centre supports parents and professionals in their efforts to assist young children to communicate effectively, and to rise to new heights. Hanen's mission is to increase knowledge and provide training to help families and professionals develop a child's best possible language, social, and literacy skills. Described here are the major programs the Centre offers to families, speech-language pathologists, early childhood educators, family support professionals, and healthcare professionals.

The first program, "It takes two to talk", has as its goal to enable parents to become their child's primary language facilitator, consequently enhancing opportunities for the development of communication in everyday situations. The objectives of the program are parent education, early language intervention, and social support.

"Learning language and loving it" is a research-based developmental approach to promoting children's social, language, and literacy development. Designed for early childhood educators whose students include children with language delays or disorders, the program is applicable to a variety of settings including childcare, preschool, nursery school, and kindergarten. The program offers training that aids teachers (a) in preventing language delays, or providing early language intervention to children with identified disorders, by creating a language-rich, highly interactive environment, or (b) in building upon the existing language skills of typically developing children.

The program for parents of late talkers, "Target word", teaches families how to facilitate expressive language development during everyday routines and activities.

For parents of children on the autism spectrum, *More than words* provides practical tools with which to help children communicate. The program emphasizes everyday activities as the context for learning to communicate, incorporating current best practice guidelines, underscoring the importance of affect, predictability, structure, and the use of visual supports to enhance learning in children with autism. The four major goals of the program are:

- improved two-way interaction
- more mature and conventional ways of communicating
- better skills in communicating for social purposes
- an improved understanding of language.

These goals and strategies, to be implemented in the home, are elaborated upon in the book, *More Than Words* (Sussman 2004). The book, published by the Hanen Centre, is a primary resource for our discussion on routines, which follows next.

Routines

Daily routines, such as dressing, mealtime, or getting ready for school, can be shaped into repetitive interactions that help children make sense of their world and improve the way they comprehend, express, predict, and behave (Sussman 2004). Because one of the defining characteristics of autism is resistance to changes in routine, frequently to the extent of insistence upon following rigid individualized rituals, it may be an effective strategy to incorporate the use of appropriate routines into a child's daily activities. The expected outcome is a structured environment that increases calm behavior, attention, and responsiveness to learning, particularly essential for children with autism and other developmental disabilities. The degree of structure required is dependent upon the needs of the child, diagnosis, age, and abilities, and is essentially more effective when coupled with routines and visual supports. The reader may refer to Chapters 4 and 6, where we presented research that supports strategies based on utilizing visual supports, engineering the environment, and following routines. Because of the previous coverage of these topics, only a brief discussion of routines will be included here.

In order to build work skills and create a comfortable learning environment educators must develop and teach within routines. Just as routines are effective in teaching functional, leisure, and vocational skills at school, they are equally relevant to the home environment. It is suggested that families build routines into everyday activities such as bathing, setting the table, or getting dressed. Doing so provides the predictability children with autism crave. The Hanen Centre's approach to structuring routines, known as the ROCK Approach, consists of the following steps.

R. *Repeat* what you say and do when you start the routine, during the routine, and when ending the routine.

O. Offer *opportunities* for the child to take turns by planning when to offer a turn, planning what turns the child can take, and offering new opportunities for turn taking, upon progressing.

C. *Cue* the child to take turns by using visual aids and engineering the situation.

K. *Keep it fun* and keep it going (Sussman 2004).

Routines are to be segmented into small steps, directed at the child's level of cognition and communication. Although the ROCK approach was designed for use by families, it can be applied just as effectively to the school setting. TEACCH (2006) also supports the use of routines and offers suggestions for their use in enhancing communication skills. According to this organization, the two reasons for using communication are (a) to regulate others and get needs met, and (b) to share attention and experiences with others. Using routines is beneficial because they are of high interest to children with autism who seek predictability, who learn they can share experiences with others and have fun while doing so, and who learn that communication is part of the process.

To be successful, it is advisable to teach routines in a meaningful and functional context, use the child's interests and strengths, set up the environment, and then introduce the activity. In the previous chapters on visual strategies and structuring the environment, we first described how to integrate the use of routines into a child's daily activities, in order to improve communication, behavior, and predictability.

Chileda

Chileda was selected for inclusion in this chapter, not because it is a one-of-a-kind organization, but rather because it typifies the kind of comprehensive vision, mission, and services that we adopt. Chileda provides services to children and young adults who have developmental disabilities, mental retardation, seizure disorders, cerebral palsy, autism, physical handicaps, genetic liabilities, or challenging behavior disorders. The members of Chileda are committed to the progressive education and personal empowerment of children with developmental disabilities, and focused on meeting individual needs and assisting clients to realize their fullest potential.

Chileda offers residential, vocational, respite, outreach, evaluation, day school, summer school, and emergency care support, through the following programs:

- Special education.
- Vocational services.
- Occupational therapy.
- Speech and language pathology.
- Physical education and physical therapy.
- Creative arts.
- A 60-day to 9-month assessment program (SNAP).

Because of synergy with our views on utilizing visual supports, structuring the environment, and enhancing communication, Chileda's list of ten of the most effective strategies for teaching students with autism spectrum disorders serves as the model for the following classroom approaches.

1. Use visual schedules to make daily routines predictable, with clear expectations.

2. Consider visual and auditory stimulation in the classroom environment.

3. Structure the environment visually, assisting children to see clearly and understand expectations, through use of defined work stations and boundaries, with cues indicating what and how much work needs to be done, when the work will be finished, and what to do next.

4. Use an AAC system for non-verbal children, such as PECS, SGDs, or communication binders.

5. Provide direct instruction in social skills, to include social stories.

6. Begin literacy instruction at an early age, as a support to communication and SGD use.

7. Complete a sensory profile to create and implement sensory integration and a sensory diet.

8. Offer a program that is consistent daily, with clear expectations.

9. Build upon students' strengths and interests.

10. Develop a strong functional curriculum that emphasizes daily living skills, community skills, recreation, leisure, and employment; and functional academics for students in an inclusive setting.

With collaboration among all team members, these strategies may be modified and implemented at home as well as at school. The methods have been discussed throughout this book, and it is anticipated that this comprehensive list will be a useful reminder of how to acquire knowledge, implement strategies, and then rise above the fear factor frequently associated with caring for or educating children with autism and other developmental disabilities or challenges to learning.

The S.U.C.C.E.S.S. approach^{SM}

The Strategic Use of Critical Curriculum Elicits Supported Sense-making (S.U.C.C.E.S.S.) utilizes a transdisciplinary approach to meeting a child's individual needs (Scotese-Wojtila, n.d.). Teams of therapists and educators work together to treat the *whole* child who seeks to connect with the world. Because children with autism spectrum or PDD display complex behaviors, they require an approach that integrates theories and strategies from a realm of perspectives (Scotese-Wojtila). For the S.U.C.C.E.S.S. Approach to be of value, the team must (a) be able to communicate effectively among members, (b) apply methods consistently across disciplines, and (c) share theoretical perspectives among interventionists. In addition to both listening and asking questions, team members must also be willing to cross train, role release, and respect the point of view of others.

During treatment of children with autism spectrum or PDD, team members serve each child differently, respecting individual learning styles rather than adhering to a particular doctrine. The child is viewed as a dynamic, complex, developing individual. With a strong emphasis on communication, children learn not only how to act, but also how to interact and learn about themselves, others, and the environment.

In Phase I of the S.U.C.C.E.S.S. Approach, a variety of interventionists (e.g. psychologist; speech, occupational, physical, music therapists; and special education teacher) work collaboratively to assess a child's needs and develop treatment strategies. Families are encouraged to observe and practice the approach during clinic visits.

In Phase II, visits to the clinic decrease as children require less therapy, and families are better equipped to apply the learned techniques at home. In the final Phase III, fewer sessions are necessary, as families become empowered with the tools to carry over strategies and apply them confidently in the home. The underpinning of the S.U.C.C.E.S.S. Approach is the recognition that autism doesn't just affect the child; rather, autism has a profound effect on the entire family. We value the approach as an effective method of reducing the fear factor, by educating and training families and school personnel to treat the child as an individual human being, with particular interests and needs, using a transdisciplinary method.

Further reading on sensory integration

Dempsey, I. and Foreman, P. (2001) "A review of educational approaches for individuals with autism." *International Journal of Disability, Development and Education 48*, 1, 103–116.

Hatch-Rasmussen, C. (1995) *Sensory Integration.* San Diego, CA: Autism Research Institute. Available at www.autism.com/families/therapy/si.html, accessed on 30 April 2010.

Mailloux, Z. and Smith Roley, S. (2001) "Sensory integration." In H. Miller-Kuhaneck (ed.) *Autism: A Comprehensive Occupational Therapy Approach.* Bethesda, MD: The American Occupational Therapy Association, Inc., pp.101–131.

Ohio Center for Autism and Low Incidence (OCALI) *Sensory Processing 101: Implications of Sensory Challenges in ASD.* Available at www.ocali.org/view.php?nav_id=101, accessed on 26 June 2009.

Parham, L.D. and Primeau, L.A. (1997) "Play and occupational therapy." In L. Parham and L. Fazio (eds) *Play in Occupational Therapy for Children.* St. Louis, MO: Mosby. pp.2–21.

Further reading on ABA

Chiesa, M. (1994) *Radical Behaviorism: The Philosophy and the Science.* Sarasota, FL: Authors Cooperative Inc., p.241.

Dawson, M. (2004) *The Misbehavior of Behaviourists: Ethical Challenges to the Autism-ABA Industry.* Available at www.sentex.net/~nexus23/naa_aba.html, accessed on 28 October 2009.

Saffran, R. (2007) *What is Applied Behavior Analysis?* Available at www.rsaffran.tripod.com/whatisaba.html#more, accessed on 23 October 2009.

Shook, G.L. and Neisworth, J.T. (2005) "Ensuring appropriate qualifications for applied behavior analyst professionals: the behavior analyst certification board." *Exceptionality 13*, 1, 3–10.

Simpson R.L. (2001) "ABA and students with autism spectrum disorders: issues and considerations for effective practice." *Focus on Autism and Other Developmental Disabilities 16*, 2, 68–71.

Wallin, J. (2004) *An Introduction to the Discrete Trial.* Available at www.polyxo.com/discretetrial, accessed on 30 April 2010.

Autism Treatment Info (2005) What is a Discrete Trial? Available at www.autismtreatment.info/What+is+a+Discrete+Trial.aspx, accessed on 10 May 2010.

Further reading

Chileda Organization (2005) *10 Effective Ways to Teach an ASD Child.* Accessed 14 September 2008.

Scotese-Wojtila, L. (2003) The S.U.C.C.E.S.S Approach. Available at www.awetismproductions.com, accessed on 1 May 2010.

Sussman, F. (2004) *More Than Words.* Toronto, ON: The Hanen Centre.

Appendix 1
National organizations

We do not endorse these organizations, but include their websites for the convenience of our readers. It is to the discretion of the reader to determine their value or worth.

Australia

Australian Advisory Board on Autism Spectrum Disorders

This board establishes and lobbies for appropriate policies to ensure the needs of individuals with autism spectrum disorder (ASD) are met. They are staunch advocates for the needs of individuals with autism, and distribute pertinent information about issues surrounding ASD.

c/o 41 Cook Street Forestville
NSW 2087
Australia
Telephone: +61 (0)2 8977 8300
www.autismaus.com.au/

Autism Aspergers Advocacy Australia (A4)

A4 is a national grassroots organization for individuals with autism and their families, promoting a national autism spectrum disorder policy and priorities. Its network of people communicate via email and the Internet, conduct activities targeting autism/ASD awareness and policy in the federal government, and complement the work of the Australian Advisory Board on Autism Spectrum Disorders, and give voice to advocacy for autism.

www.a4.org.au/a4/node/7

Autism Association of Western Australia

They pledge to provide for the needs and interests of individuals with autism by offering services based on evidence-based research. Their mission is to promote community involvement and enhance individual and social growth.

37 Hay Street
Subiaco 6008
Australia
http://www.autism.org.au/

Autism Spectrum Australia (Aspect)

They are committed to offering services to individuals with autism of all ages. They utilize evidence-based approaches to ensure quality and effective interventions, services, and information.

Forrestville
NSW 2087
Australia
Telephone: 1-800-069978
www.autismspectrum.org.au

Canada

Autism Awareness Centre, Inc.

This global website offers links to Canada, Europe, Global, United Kingdom, and the United States. Visitors to the Canada link may click on a province or territory on the map shown to find autism help in their area. Each country lists organizations, professionals, research centers, projects, and various aspects related to services provided to individuals with autism and their families and caregivers, and healthcare providers. Blogs, newsletters, conferences are included.

www.autismawarenesscentre.com

Autism Canada Foundation

The intent of this organization is to engage, educate, and unite people to find a cure for autism. The Autism Canada Foundation supports Canadians by providing biomedical and behavioral treatment information to help those affected by autism, expand the knowledge of healthcare professionals, influence governmental policy, and enable research into causes and treatment for autism. The website offers current findings on these topics, as well as opportunities to get involved, a calendar of events, and other areas of interest.

www.autismcanada.org

Autism Society Canada

ASC's website provides visitors with reliable information on autism and referrals to helpful services and resources, whether sought by a person with an autism spectrum disorder, parent, caregiver, volunteer, researcher, educator, or healthcare or social services professional. ASC places a special emphasis on families seeking support for children with autism, and aims to assist with making successful community connections, information dissemination, and providing whatever families need to ensure people with ASD reach their full potential as participating members of their communities.

www.autismsocietycanada.ca/index_e.html

Ministry of Children and Family Development-Autism Initiatives Branch

This British Columbia government agency provides early behavioral intervention, autism funding for children under age six and those aged 6–18 years. Information included on this website offers community resources and programs, publications, leisure and recreational opportunities, and news related to those affected by autism spectrum disorders.

www.mcf.gov.bc.ca/autism

United Kingdom

Autism Initiative UK

Addresses the unique abilities of individuals with autism to establish individualized needs and provide support through a range of services.

7 Chesterfield Road
Liverpool
Merseyside
L23 9XL
UK
Telephone: 0151 330 9500
www.autisminitiatives.org/

Autism Services Directory

An all-inclusive resource where individuals with autism, caregivers, and professionals may locate services and supports that may address their specific needs.

www.autism.org.uk/en-gb/directory.aspx

Derbyshire Autism Services Group

The Derbyshire Autism Services Group (D.A.S.G.) is a parent-led registered charity that utilizes a volunteer board of directors and members. The members are from a variety of backgrounds enabling them to provide priceless services to individuals with autism spectrum disorders, care givers, as well as professionals. The services D.A.S.G. offer include support groups, family events, trainings/inservices, short-term respite care, social skills training, and advice.

28D High Street
Ripley
Derbyshire
DE5 3HH
UK
Telephone: (01773) 741221
E-mail: dasg@autismssupport.co.uk
www.autismsupport.co.uk/default.asp

The National Autism Society

The National Autism Society is the most prominent charity for individuals with autism in the UK. Comprehensive services are provided to assist individuals seeking information, support, and increased public awareness about the needs for individuals with autism. This website offers caregivers information, advice, support, and individualized assessment of their needs. The individual with autism may receive education/vocational training opportunities, social skills training, and assistance in gaining employment.

http://www.autism.org.uk/

Research Autism

A cumulative directory of autism research exclusive to the topics of interventions for education, social skills, health and other areas are offered.

Westbourne House
14-16 Westbourne Grove
London
W2 5RH
UK
Telephone: 020 7317 5785
www. researchautism.net/

The UK Autism Foundation

A British autism charity providing comprehensive information about the latest research and news on the topic of autism. The foundation is looking to establish an unprecedented Autism Centre in London to educate individuals with autism and create provisions for those needing financial assistance to access appropriate training.

Woodford Business Centre
113-115 George Lane
South Woodford
London
E18 1AB
UK
Telephone: 020 8989 4810
www.ukautismfoundation.org/

USA

Asperger Syndrome Education Network ASPEN

A national non-profit organization providing education and support to families and individuals affected by Asperger syndrome, PDD-NOS, high-functioning autism, and related disorders.

9 Aspen Circle
Edison
NJ 08820
Tel: +1 (732) 321 0880
www.aspennj.org

Association for Behavior Analysis International (ABAI)

The ABAI promotes the experimental, theoretical, and applied analysis of behavior, encompassing contemporary scientific and social issues, theoretical advances, and the dissemination of professional and public information.

550 West Centre Avenue
Suite 1
Portage
MI 49024
Tel: +1 (269) 492 9310
www.abainternational.org

Autism Research Network

This network provides information about two major research networks dedicated to understanding and treating autism. The Collaborative Programs of Excellence in Autism (CPEA) network conducts research to learn about the possible causes of autism, including genetics, immunological, and environmental factors, as well as diagnosis, early detection, behavioral and communications characteristics, and treatment of autism. The Studies to Advance Autism Research and Treatment (STAART) network focuses on the causes, diagnosis, early detection, prevention, and treatment of autism.

www.nimh.nih.gov/health/topics/autism-spectrum-disorders-pervasive-developmental-disorders/nih-initiatives/staart/index.shtml

Autism Society

The Autism Society, the nation's leading grassroots autism organization, improves the lives of all affected by autism by increasing public awareness about the day-to-day issues faced by people on the spectrum, advocating for appropriate services for individuals across the lifespan, and providing the latest information regarding treatment, education, research, and advocacy.

4340 East-West Highway
Suite 650
Bethesda
MD 20814
Tel: +1 (301) 657 0881
www.autism-society.org

Autism Speaks

Autism Speaks' goal is to change the future for all who struggle with ASDs. It is dedicated to funding global biomedical research into the causes, prevention, treatments, and cure for autism; raising public awareness about autism and its effects on individuals, families, and society; and bringing hope to all who deal with the hardships of this disorder.

2 Park Avenue
11th Floor
New York
NY 10016
Tel: +1 (212) 252 8584
www.autismspeaks.org

Autism Treatment Network

An online global resource with main links to the Autism Treatment, Autism Society, Children with Autism, Autism Diagnosis, Autism Spectrum, and Autism Resources. Related searches may be made on a number of topics, to acquire comprehensive information related to autism spectrum disorders.

www.autismtreatmentnetwork.org

Centers for Disease Control and Prevention (CDC)

CDC's mission is to collaborate to create the expertise, information, and tools that people and communities need to protect their health— through health promotion, prevention of disease, injury and disability, and preparedness for new health threats.

1600 Clifton Road
Atlanta
GA 30333
Tel: +1 (800) 232 4636
www.CDC.gov

Developmental Disabilities Clinic at the Yale Child Study Center

The autism program, an interdisciplinary group of clinicians and scholars, provides comprehensive clinical services to children with ASDs and their families. One of the leading research centers in the world, Yale was recently recognized as a National Institute of Health autism center of excellence. The program involves individuals with autism and related disorders, and integrates highly experienced professionals from the fields of clinical psychology, neuropsychology and neuroimaging, child psychiatry, speech-language pathology, social work, genetics, and the biological sciences, as well as psychopharmacology and psychiatric nursing. .

Yale University
230 South Frontage Road
New Haven
CT 06520
Tel: +1 (203) 785 3420
www.childstudycenter.yale.edu/autism

Family Center on Technology and Disability (FCTD)

This Center is a resource to support organizations and programs that work with families of children and youth with disabilities. It offers a range of information and services on assistive technologies. Network members are committed to providing useful information and resources to help children fulfill their potential and ensure members receive the most current information on developments in the field of assistive technology.

Academy for Educational Development (AED)
1825 Connecticut Avenue NW
7th Floor
Washington
DC 20009-5721
Tel: +1 (202)884 8068
www.fctd.info

Gray Center

The Gray Center is a non-profit organization that strives to assist individuals with autism spectrum disorder (ASD) and their communicative partners with a mutual understanding of social learning. It is the goal of the Gray Center to create more effective communication exchanges by equipping both the individuals with ASD and those who interact with them with information and strategies about social differences and why they occur. The individual with ASD gains an improved understanding of social rules and the reasons for them. Those who interact with this person gain a clearer understanding of their perspective. In their efforts to promote social understanding, members of the Gray Center provide many worthwhile resources that benefit individuals with autism and others who work alongside them.

100 Pine Street
Suite 121
Zeeland
MI 49464
Tel: +1 (616) 748 6030
www.thegraycenter.org

Indiana Resource Center for Autism (IRCA)

This Center conducts outreach training and consultations, engages in research, and develops and disseminates information on behalf of individuals across the autism spectrum. Efforts are focused on providing communities, organizations, agencies, and families with knowledge and skills to support children and adults in typical early intervention, school, community, work, and home settings.

Indiana Institute on Disability and Community
2853 E. 10th Street
Bloomington
IN 47408-2696
Tel: +1 (812) 855 6508
www.iidc.indiana.edu/irca

Interactive Autism Network (IAN)

IAN is an innovative online project designed to accelerate the pace of autism research by linking researchers and families. Anyone affected by an ASD can become part of IAN's online community to stay informed about autism research, provide feedback, and make their voices heard.

www.ianproject.org

Learning Disabilities Association of America (LDA)

LDA is a national network of state-based advocacy groups for families affected by learning disabilities. It has been very supportive of issues surrounding some of the learning difficulties common to children with severe social disability, such as those characterized by non-verbal learning disability (NLD).

4156 Library Road
Pittsburgh
PA 15234-1349
Tel: +1 (412) 341 1515
www.ldanatl.org

National Autism Center

The National Autism Center is a new non-profit organization dedicated to supporting effective, evidence-based treatment approaches and providing direction to families, practitioners, organizations, policy makers, and funders. The Center is bringing nationally renowned experts together to establish national treatment standards, model best practices, and conduct applied research, thereby serving as a vital source of information, training, and services.
41 Pacella Park Drive
Randolph
MA 02368
Tel: +1 (877) 313 3833
www.nationalautismcenter.org

National Dissemination Center for Children with Disabilities (NICHCY)

This Center serves the nation as a central source of information on:
* disabilities in infants, toddlers, children, and youth
* The Individuals with Disabilities Education Improvement Act (IDEA) 2004, which is the law authorizing special education
* The No Child Left Behind (NCLB) Act 2001 (as it relates to children with disabilities)
* research-based information on effective educational practices.
1825 Connecticut Avenue NW
Suite 700
Washington
DC 20009
Tel: +1 (202) 884 8200
www.nichcy.org

Online Asperger Syndrome Information and Support (OASIS)

The Online Asperger Syndrome Information and Support (OASIS) center has joined with MAAP Services for Autism and Asperger Syndrome to serve as a single resource and support for families, individuals, and medical professionals who deal with the challenges of Asperger Syndrome, autism, and other pervasive development disabilities (PDD).

More advanced individuals with Autism, Asperger's syndrome, and Pervasive developmental disorder (MAAP) are served by a non-profit organization providing information and advice to families. Through The MAAP, its quarterly newsletter, parents and professionals network with others in similar circumstances and learn about more advanced individuals within the autism spectrum.

The website includes featured articles support boards, blogs, chatrooms, and other comprehensive information.

www.aspergersyndrome.org

Professional Development in Autism (PDA) Center

This Center provides training and consulting to school teams that work with students with ASD from diagnosis through age 21. The goal is to increase the capacity of school teams so every child with ASD can access a high-quality public education.

Locations: University of Washington, University of Colorado at Denver, Maryland Coalition for Inclusive Education, University of South Florida, and University of Oklahoma.

www.depts.washington.edu/pdacent

TalkAutism

TalkAutism is a communication service used by many organizations which share a common database of resource directories, distance learning libraries, and special message boards.

Box 1348
Princeton
NJ 08540
Tel: +1 (888) 355 7161
www.talkautism.org

Technical Assistance Center on Positive Behavioral Interventions and Supports (PBIS)

This Center, founded by the Office of Special Education Programs (OSEP) was established to address the behavioral and discipline systems needed for successful learning and social development of students. It provides capacity-building information and technical support about behavioral systems to assist states and districts in the design of effective schools.

www.pbis.org

Treatment and Education of Autistic and related Communication Handicapped Children (TEACCH)

TEACCH utilizes an approach for treatment that focuses on the person with autism and the development of a program around the individual's skills, interests, and needs. TEACCH provides clinical services, conducts training, and provides consultation for teachers, residential care providers, and other professionals. Research activities include psychological, educational, and biomedical studies. Administrative headquarters are in Chapel Hill, North Carolina.

Tel: +1 (919) 966 2174
www.teacch.com

Global websites

Action for Autism (AFA)

AFA is the pioneering, national and non-profit autism society of India, providing support and services to individuals with autism, their families, and those who work with them in South Asia. The mission of AFA is to facilitate a barrier-free environment, empower families of persons with autism, and to act as a catalyst for change, enabling their full participation as contributing members of the community. Research, training, events, referrals, education and information dissemination are located on the website and offered by the organization.

www.autism-india.org/afa_autisminindia.html

Autism Organizations Worldwide

This website, maintained by Action for Autism, India, is an alphabetical list of mostly national and some regional autism organizations. Direct links to individual contacts and addresses are listed and actively updated to provide the most recent information on autism for children and their families to over 100 sites.

www.autism-india.org/worldorgs.html

Appendix 2
Goals and Objectives

Chapter 1: Speech Generating Devices (SGDs)

GOAL: Using a speech generating device (SGD), the child will relay basic needs, wants, or information, during structured activities at home and at school.

OBJECTIVES: Using an SGD, the child will do the following:

- Communicate at least five simple messages (e.g. need to use the bathroom, hungry, more, finished) ____% of the time, during ____ opportunities.

- Choose a free-time activity (e.g. computers, reading area, puzzles, manipulatives, TV, rest) upon request ____% of the time, during ____ opportunities.

- Independently communicate requests during meal or snack time (e.g. more or no more, help, choices of food) ____% of the time.

- Independently request materials needed to complete a structured art activity (e.g. crayon, scissors, glue, paper) ____% of the time, during ____ opportunities.

- Refrain from using negative behaviors and use device to gain the attention of a communicative partner ____% of the time, while in the classroom, home, or community setting.

- Identify peers and adults in structured group or play activities with____% accuracy.

- Label at least _____ items from each of the categories of foods, animals, clothing, colors, shapes, school supplies, and common items, with ____% accuracy.

- Use the appropriate vocabulary _____% of the time when describing given action pictures.

- Use the appropriate preposition _____% of the time when describing spatial location of objects during structured activities.

Chapter 2: Picture Exchange Communication System (PECS)

GOAL: The child will communicate basic wants, needs, and simple messages independently, in both school and home settings.

OBJECTIVES: Given the PECS, as recommended by Frost and Bondy (2002), the child will do the following:

- Upon seeing a desired item or object, and with a picture of it within reach, pick up the picture, reach to the person holding the item who is within 1 foot (33cm), and release the picture into that person's hand independently _____% of the time.

- Upon seeing a desired item or object, and with a picture of it alone on a communication book within reach, remove the picture from the book, seek out the communication partner who is within (1 foot; 33cm) (5 feet; 2m) (10 feet; 4m) (across the room) away, and give the picture to complete requests independently _____% of the time.

- Upon seeing a desired item or object, and with a picture of it alone on a communication book, go to the book that is (1 foot; 33cm) (5 feet; 2m) (10 feet; 4m) (across the room) away, remove the picture, move to the communication partner, and give the picture to complete requests independently _____% of the time.

- Upon seeing a desired item or object, and with a picture of it on a communication book, along with a picture of a distracter item, give the communication partner the correct picture. (a) Give the correct picture _____% of the time (b) Give the correct picture _____% of the time when the book and partner are more than 2 feet (66 cm) away.

- Upon seeing a variety of reinforcing items, go to the communication book, select an appropriate picture from all those available (on the cover or inside), remove and give the picture to the communication partner, and then, when told to "Go ahead and get it", retrieve the corresponding item independently _____% of the time.

- With reinforcing items not in sight, go to the communication book, select a picture from any page within it, remove and give the picture to the communication partner, and then, when told to "Go ahead and get it," get the corresponding item independently ____% of the time, across a variety of objects, activities, communication partners, and environments.

- Given a communication book with a variety of pictures and a sentence strip with an "I want" symbol attached to the left end, attach a symbol of the desired item or object to the right end of the strip. Then, give the strip to the communication partner independently ____% of the time, across a variety of objects, activities, communication partners, and environments.

- Given a communication book with a variety of pictures and a sentence strip with an "I want" symbol attached to the left end, remove the "I want" symbol and affix it to the left end of the sentence strip. Then, remove the symbol of a desirable item from the book, affix it to the right end of the sentence strip, and independently give the entire strip to the communication partner ____% of the time, across a variety of objects, activities, communication partners, and environments.

- Locate the communication book, construct an entire sentence strip, go to the communication partner, and exchange the strip for the desirable item independently ____% of the time, across a variety of objects, activities, communication partners, and environments. (Frost and Bondy 2002)

Further reading on PECS

Frost, L.A. and Bondy, A. (2002) *The Picture Exchange Communication System Training Manual.* Newark, DE: Pyramid Educational Products Inc.

Chapter 3: Symbolic Language Systems

GOAL: The child will relay basic wants and needs using an effective method of communication consistently at home, school, or in the community.

OBJECTIVES: Using a symbolic language system that has been taught and practiced (e.g. icons, photographs, sign language, gestures, vocal approximations, communication wallet, SGD), the child will do the following:

- Request a desirable item (e.g. snack, toy, activity) when prompted ____% of the time.

- Choose a free-time activity (e.g. computers, reading, puzzles, manipulatives, TV, rest) when prompted ___% of the time.

- Communicate at least five simple messages (e.g. needs to use the bathroom, hungry, more, finished) ____% of the time, during _____ opportunities.

- Communicate requests independently during meal or snack time (e.g. more or no more, help, choices of food) ____% of the time.

- Request materials needed to complete a structured art activity (e.g. crayon, scissors, glue, paper) independently ____% of the time.

- Gain the attention of a communication partner appropriately (e.g. raise icon, gesture, sign language, SGD message), while refraining from using negative behaviors ____% of the time.

- Identify peers and adults in structured group or play activities expressively, with ____% accuracy.

GOAL: The child will use appropriate vocabulary when relaying messages and sharing basic information, using an effective method of communication consistently at home, school, or in the community.

OBJECTIVES: Using a symbolic language system that has been taught and practiced (e.g. icons, photographs, sign language, gestures, vocal approximations, communication wallet, SGD), the child will do the following:

- Label at least _____ items from each category of foods, clothing, animals, household items, feelings, and body parts, with____% accuracy.

- Describe with ___% accuracy, at least ten pictures from each category of colors, shapes, and prepositions.

- Respond to ____ (number of) "who", "what", and "where" questions about ___ (number of) composite pictures, with ____% accuracy.

- Formulate sentences of at least ____ words, when describing _____ composite pictures ____% of the time.

- Use the correct pronoun or noun, verb form, and tense when describing _____ pictures ____% of the time.

- Use at least _____ words or _____ sentences to re-tell an event or story after a short delay, when given picture or verbal cues _____% of the time.

- Answer ten simple "Wh-" questions related to personal wants, needs, daily activities, or play _____% of the time, during _____ opportunities.

- Provide personal information (e.g. name, address, phone number, school) upon request _____% of the time, with _____% accuracy.

Chapter 4: Visual Supports

GOAL: The child will participate in and respond to requests and activities in the classroom or home settings appropriately.

OBJECTIVES: Given direct instruction, practice, and visual supports (e.g. Wait card, timer, picture schedule, Social Story, Count down card, Flip book, reminder strip, sign language or gestural cues), the child will do the following:

- Transition between classroom activities or home routines within _____ seconds of request _____% of the time.

- Follow simple behavioral directions (e.g. sit down, line up, hands down, clean up, quiet) _____% of the time.

- Complete at least _____ structured activities (e.g. shoebox-type activity or pre-vocational activity) independently, at individual work station _____% of the time, during _____ (minutes/hours) time periods.

- Complete an activity, put in a FINISHED container, refer to schedule to learn what to do next, and start a new activity independently _____% of the time.

- Follow at least _____ directional instructions (e.g. where to sit, wait, work, line up, play) independently _____% of the time.

- Complete three- to five-step tasks during routine activities (e.g. breakfast, arrival at school, ready for bed routine, brush teeth routine, toileting routine, hygiene routine) independently _____% of the time.

- Store belongings (e.g. coat, back pack, homework assignments, dirty clothes) independently in designated areas _____% of the time.

GOAL: The child will appropriately respond to social situations in the classroom, home, or community settings.

OBJECTIVES: Given direct instruction, practice, and visual supports (e.g. Wait card, timer, picture schedule, Social Story, Count down card, Flip book, reminder strip, sign language or gestural cues), the child will do the following:

- Demonstrate appropriate turn-taking behavior during structured group activities ____% of the time.

- Demonstrate comprehension of socially appropriate behavior by naming ____ acceptable behaviors during structured learning activities ____% of the time.

- Tolerate sharing play space with peers without engaging in inappropriate physical behaviors ____% of the time.

- Replace negative behaviors (e.g. inappropriate touching, inappropriate greetings, negative mealtime behavior, emotional outbursts) with acceptable behavior ____% of the time, during structured social activities.

- Initiate conversation and maintain topic when responding to statements and answering simple questions ____% of the time.

- Participate appropriately in ____ life skill activities (e.g. phone manners, table manners, interactions with strangers, interactions with visitors) ____% of the time.

- Remain with the group when transitioning through the educational or community setting ____% of the time.

Chapter 5: Social Stories

GOAL: The child will respond appropriately to and interact in structured social situations in the classroom, home, or community settings.

OBJECTIVES: Given a Social Story describing desired behaviors, presented consistently, the child will do the following:

- Display appropriate attention-getting behaviors (e.g. gesture, SGD message, raised icon) ____% of the time.

- Reduce inappropriate noises at school and home ____% of the time.

- Greet others appropriately ____% of the time.

- Respond appropriately to questions and comments of others _____% of the time.

- Comply with safety directions (e.g. stay with the group, watch for cars, listen to a familiar adult, don't leave with a stranger) _____% of the time.

Chapter 6: Structured Environments

GOAL: The child will complete work tasks, and follow rules and routines independently at home and in school.

OBJECTIVES: Given direct instruction, practice, and visual supports (e.g. Wait card, timer, picture schedule, Social Story, Count down card, Flip book, reminder strip, sign language or gestural cues), the child will do the following:

- Move to an area to reorganize self with needed sensory input _____% of the time, given a designated calming area to prevent an escalation of inappropriate behaviors.

- Transition between areas in the classroom or at home within _____ seconds of request _____% of the time.

- Transition independently to an appropriate area (e.g. locker, work station, restroom) _____% of the time.

- Remain in designated area (e.g. circle time area, work station, rest area) for _____ minutes _____% of the time, provided there are structural barriers.

- Independently complete _____ structured tasks that are located in a work area _____% of the time.

- Store materials in appropriate areas at school and home _____% of the time.

- Complete routines (e.g. school arrival routine of storing belongings, given labeled areas or containers; setting dinner table, given place mat with place-setting outline; hygiene routine, brushing teeth, using deodorant, bathing) independently _____% of the time.

GOAL: The teacher or family will organize and arrange the child's environment to facilitate learning, behavior, and communication.

OBJECTIVES: The teacher or family will do the following:

- Label and provide sufficient space for work areas; label storage areas to identify where items belong.

- Remove distractions from work and rest areas.

- Make readily available and accessible the materials necessary to complete an activity (e.g. hygiene items, dishes, shoebox-type activities, structured assignments).

- Provide visual supports that indicate to the child how much work there is to do, what the work is, when it will be finished, and where to go next.

- Visually monitor the child's activities at all times.

- Display and discuss visual cues that communicate information about upcoming events (e.g. activity schedule, transition pictures, calendar).

- Make readily available and accessible, and encourage use of the child's communication system (e.g. photographs, communication binder, PECS, SGD).

Index